WHAT JUNG
Really SAID

1945-1995

50 YEARS OF PUBLISHING

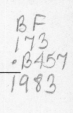

WHAT JUNG *Really* SAID

E.A. BENNET

Introduction by
ANTHONY STORR

SCHOCKEN BOOKS   NEW YORK

SCHOCKEN BOOKS, NEW YORK

Library of Congress Cataloging-in-Publication Data

Bennet, E. A. (Edward Armstrong)
What Jung really said.
Includes index.
1. Psychoanalysis. 2. Jung, C. G. (Carl Gustav), 1875–1961.
I. Title.
BF173.B457   1983   150.19 54   83–42715
ISBN 0–8052–1046–6

Manufactured in the United States of America
['95] 9 8 7 6 5 4 3 2 1

CONTENTS

INTRODUCTION

ANTHONY STORR

Carl Gustav Jung is one of those figures in psychology of whom everyone has heard, but whose writings are less familiar. If the bibliography and general index to Jung's works are included, the Collected Works consist of no less than twenty large volumes. The general reader wishing to acquaint himself with Jung's thought is likely to quail before such a large body of work, and to feel in need of guidance as to where to begin. *What Jung Really Said* provides an excellent introduction to Jung's main ideas in language which anyone can follow. The late E. A. Bennet was a personal friend of Jung's, and often stayed with him and his family in Zurich. They exchanged ideas both in letters and in personal meetings over many years, so that what Dr. Bennet has to say has an authenticity unmatched by other accounts of Jung and his work.

Jung was born in 1875 and died in 1961. Many of his ideas and some of the terms he introduced have become incorporated into psychology without recognition of their origin. Jung was the first to apply psychoanalytic ideas to the study of schizophrenia. He introduced the concepts of *extraversion* and *introversion,* and the terms *complex, archetype, individuation,* and *collective unconscious.* Jung's notion of the mind as a self-regulating system accords well with modern ideas in physiology and cybernetics. His insistence that man needed to search for meaning in his life anticipated the views of the existentialists. Yet Jung's importance tends to be underestimated, and those who have not troubled to read his

1

writings often dismiss him as a visionary mystic whose work is so out of line with experimental psychology that it can be safely ignored. In fact, as his early research demonstrates, Jung had a competent grasp of scientific method; but the bulk of his later work is concerned with areas in which scientific method cannot be applied. The meaning of life cannot be quantified, but this does not invalidate man's search for meaning. Today, when psychological laboratories throughout the world are dominated by the experimental approach, Jung's insistence that the subjective experience of the individual is vitally significant is a valuable counterbalance. Jung believed that individual self-knowledge and self-development, together with the enhanced capacity for relationships with others which accompanies this development, were the only factors strong enough to resist the collective dominance of the State. This is what he meant when he stated that the individual was the carrier of culture. The whole thrust of Jungian analysis is toward helping the individual to realize his potentialities, toward facilitating his becoming more authentically himself. Jung was not concerned with statistical "normality" nor with adaptation to society's expectations. Many of his analytic patients were conventionally successful people with considerable achievements already behind them, but who had found that such achievements brought little sense of fulfillment. Faced with patients of this kind, Jung proffered no ready solutions, but encouraged them to explore the inner world of dream and phantasy. By paying serious attention to what was going on within, the individual could be enabled to rediscover aspects of his own nature which had been neglected or overlaid, and thus find again the path of his own authentic development. Jung named this quest for personal authenticity the "process of individuation."

I have elsewhere described individuation as "a kind of

Pilgrim's Progress without a creed, aiming not at heaven, but at integration and wholeness." For Jung, analysis was a spiritual quest; a deeply serious endeavor to come to terms with oneself, to accept oneself, and to become, as far as possible, the person which it was intended one should be. The parallels with the self-examination and spiritual exercises enjoined by religious disciplines are clear. Jung himself was a deeply religious man, but also so profoundly unorthodox that he shocked both Protestant and Catholic theologians. His own, individual point of view was only achieved at the cost of a good deal of pain and a profound mental upheaval which, at one time, threatened to overwhelm him.

Jung was born and brought up in Switzerland. The greater part of his childhood was passed near Basel, in which city he went to school from the age of eleven. Later he studied medicine at the University of Basel. Jung's father was a clergyman, a pastor in the Swiss Reformed Church, and there were six parsons in his mother's family. From an early age, Jung was exposed to a great deal of religious discussion and practice. But, as he records in his autobiography, even in childhood, he experienced visions and dreams of a religious kind which did not fit in with the conventional teachings of the Church. His attempts to discuss his doubts with his father were always repudiated; for, although his father was kind and well-disposed toward him, he was also content to accept the system of religious belief in which he had been reared and was unwilling to consider any alternative. Jung had to keep his unorthodoxy to himself, but remained true to his own vision in spite of the guilt and sense of alienation from his family which this entailed.

In 1900, Jung began his career in psychiatry by becoming an assistant physician to Eugen Bleuler at the Burghölzli mental hospital in Zurich. He wrote a dissertation for his

M.D., and carried out a great deal of experimental work with patients, using the so-called word-association tests. By means of these tests, Jung was able to demonstrate objectively that individuals were influenced by mental contents of which they were entirely unaware. It was the first experimental demonstration of Freud's concept of repression. In 1907, Jung published a book on schizophrenia which owed much to Freud's ideas, and which he sent to Freud. As Dr. Bennet recalls, it was this which led to the two men meeting. Their collaboration lasted until 1913.

Although Jung always acknowledged his debt to Freud, he was never an uncritical disciple. It must be remembered that Freud, working in his private office, had virtually no experience of psychotic patients; whereas Jung's chief concern, while he was working in the Burghölzli, was with cases of schizophrenia. It is not surprising that the two men developed different models of the mind. Jung records in his autobiography that, when he was working on the book which was eventually titled *Symbols of Transformation,* he realized that to publish it would cost him Freud's friendship. This proved to be the case. Their parting, which can be traced in the Freud/Jung letters, was bitter: and led to Jung's experiencing so severe a mental upheaval that he feared that he was "menaced by a psychosis."

When Jung was a child, he had rebelled against the dogmas of the Church, and had felt compelled to be true to his own vision. In mid-life, he felt compelled to rebel against the dogmas of Freud, and to hold true to his own conception of psychology. During the years of the First World War, Jung engaged in a process of self-analysis which he called "Confrontation with the Unconscious." He emerged from this period of storm and stress with renewed strength and the conviction that, come what might, he had to trust his own experience and bear witness to the insights that he had gained.

As Jung himself affirmed, the foundations of his particular point of view were laid in the years during which he was driven in upon himself. At the time of his parting with Freud, Jung was thirty-eight years old. His insistence that the mid-life period was a kind of turning point in psychological development took origin from his own experience. It is because of that experience that Jung's major contribution to psychology concerns the field of adult development. Jung was well aware of the importance of early childhood in determining adult personality. In the case of young people whose main problem was a failure to emancipate themselves from the family, Jung advised analysis along the lines laid down by Freud or Adler. But the cases which really interested him, and to whose treatment he made an important contribution, were people who, in the mid-life period, had begun to find life sterile or futile. Jung referred to this type of neurosis as "getting stuck," meaning by this that the natural course of the person's development had become arrested. In Jung's view, the neurotic symptoms which drove people to seek analysis were often valuable indications that they were straying from their own true path of development, rather than aberrations to be abolished by treatment. Jung would sometimes say, "Thank God he became neurotic," implying that anxiety and depression and other symptoms of mental distress could be seen in a positive light, as pointers indicating to the sufferer that a re-examination of his values and way of life was urgently required. Jung's study of people of this kind led him to conclude that "getting stuck" was usually the result of a one-sided attitude to life which had cramped the individual's development. The extravert tended to be too exclusively concerned with the external world, while the introvert neglected the external world and failed to adapt to it. The task of analysis was to restore the balance and thus allow normal development to proceed.

Jung thought that the psyche was a self-regulating system. By exploring the world of dream and phantasy, the patient could be put in touch with the unconscious, which was striving to compensate and correct his one-sided conscious attitude. Jungian analysis is orientated more toward the future than toward the past. The most important way of getting in touch with the unconscious is by dream analysis. Jung's view of dreams was very different from that of Freud. He did not accept Freud's idea that dreams were invariably an indirect way of giving expression to forbidden wishes. Jung thought of dreams as communications from the unconscious which, being couched in symbolic language, might be hard to understand, but which were not necessarily concealing the unacceptable. Commonly, dreams were compensatory to the conscious point of view; expressions of aspects of the individual which were neglected or unrealized. Some particularly impressive dreams contained visions and ideas of deep significance, which could not be accounted for in term's of the individual's past experience, but seemed to spring from a source outside the range of personal contrivance. Such dreams gave expression to "archetypal" images which could be found in myths and fairy tales from different cultures all over the world. It was such phenomena which led Jung to postulate a deeper level of mind than the merely personal, which he named the "collective unconscious."

As he records in his autobiography, Jung was deeply influenced by Kant and Schopenhauer, whom he had read while still an adolescent. Jung came to believe that space and time were human categories imposed upon reality which did not accurately reflect it. The same might be true of the categories "physical" and "mental." One of Jung's collaborators was the famous physicist Wolfgang Pauli. Jung came to think that the physicist's investigation of matter and the psychologist's investigation of mind might in fact be different ways of approaching the same reality. Perhaps mind and body were artificial divisions; different aspects of a single reality perceived through different frames of reference. Jung's belief in the ultimate unity of all existence is an important determinant of his thought.

Whether or not one shares Jung's fundamental beliefs, there can be no doubt of the importance of his many contributions to the study of the mind. His emphasis upon the spiritual aspects of human nature provides a needed contrast with Freud's insistence upon the physical. Jung's affirmation of the importance of self-realization as a goal, and his certainty that the highest achievements of mankind are always individual achievements stand as challenges to political and social systems which exalt the State at the expense of the individual. Dr. Bennet's book will continue to provide a valuable service by introducing Jung's thought to a wide circle of readers.

THE COLLECTED
WORKS OF C.G. JUNG

London: Routledge & Kegan Paul.
Princeton, N.J.: Bollingen Foundation.

* Not yet published.

FOREWORD

C. G. Jung's contributions to psychology and psychiatry appeared in a fairly steady stream for nearly sixty years, that is, from his first publication in 1902, till 1961, the year in which he died. A complete edition of his Collected Works in English is in process of publication. He had an original mind and from the first his books attracted attention. Of special interest to him was the everyday adaptation of the individual to others. This natural, healthy contact between people was not so simple as it looked; often inability to communicate with others was noticed in patients whose minds were disturbed.

As his work matured he saw evidence that the mind, like the body, in addition to personal features, had collective contents which, to quote Jung, "are peculiar not to one individual, but to many at the same time, i.e. either to a society, a people, or to mankind in general".[1] This opened up new territory and produced a lot of controversy. Certainly it was a daring hypothesis; but Jung held that no advance in knowledge was possible without some hypothesis and he did not attempt to prove every theory he put forward before applying it empirically in the elucidation of problems he met in his treatment of patients. His main concern was to find out all he could about the functioning of the conscious mind and from this to learn something of that part of our mind we know only by inference—the unconscious.

For Jung the symptoms of psychiatric illness were simply signs of disturbed normal functioning. Thus he was concerned more with the healthy than with the unhealthy elements in the personality. Symptoms, distressing though they may be, are often nature's effort to cure, to restore the correct, normal working of the mind. But what was normal, that is, average performance? Here was the problem. Amid the numerous signs and symptoms of mental ill-health Jung, with no preconceived ideas, set himself the task of understanding and perhaps removing some of the obscurities. Later he learnt that besides dealing with the personal disability of his patient, it might be necessary to take into account more general disturbances, such as happen during a trade slump, or a war, and sweep through a whole nation like an infection. In other words, Jung saw his patient not as an isolated individual, but as an individual in the community.

He was one of a small group of doctors who, in the early years of this century, became interested in finding out more about the mind. A lot had been written about spiritualism, psychical research, and similar subjects. Yet there was no authoritative information. An ideal opportunity of getting first-hand knowledge lay in learning about mental illness, its meaning, its causes and its treatment. Much had been done to improve the lot of the insane in this country, in France and in Germany, chiefly in providing better living conditions and kindly care. Yet no progress, or very little, had been made in understanding the mind itself. Doctors were disposed to accept as established practice that beyond institutional care, little or nothing could be done for those who had "gone mental". Such a *laissez-faire* attitude did not appeal to Jung who wanted to understand "the intruders of the mind" as he described the fears, the false ideas, the misunderstandings about life, which can destroy personal as well as family happiness and wreck so many lives.

Psychology, physiology and pharmacology have now combined in the treatment of mental disorders to an extent unheard of in the nineteenth century. Since the study of the mind was taken up seriously, the subject-matter of psychology has expanded, and its influence has spread, so that today everybody is concerned with psychology in some form or other. It is mentioned in conversation, in newspapers, in general literature. Without effort we have absorbed terms such as *extravert, introvert, complex*. Yet these were unknown in psychology until Jung introduced them. They describe features in human nature, knowledge of which is often taken for granted by the man in the street, as though it had always been an established part of our natural endowment.

In addition to his medical knowledge, Jung was a classical scholar—he read Latin and Greek almost as easily as his native tongue—and an accomplished linguist. These attainments in themselves mattered little to Jung himself. He had simple tastes, an easy, natural manner, with a fine sense of humour and a genuine interest in what others had to say—provided they had something to say and did not want to meet him merely because he was famous. He did not relish adulation or publicity, he was just himself.

No one would regard Jung as a popular writer and some of his books are stiff going. How could it be otherwise? Nature is not in the habit of revealing herself in accordance with our expectations. Jung avoided final conclusions and dogmatic pronouncements, and he made no attempt to build up a well-rounded system, in which everything fitted neatly. Knowing very well the complexity and waywardness of the human mind he retained his pioneer outlook and never felt tempted to lay down the law or claim general validity for his views. While always ready to revise his opinion, if he had good reason to do so, he never acted in a hurry but reserved his judgment. Consequently he wrote with assurance, based upon careful assessment of the facts as he found them. Often his views were misunderstood—as has happened to every great thinker—and he had his critics who disapproved or insisted on seeing life from another angle. This makes it all the more important to know what Jung really said about the key topics in modern psychological thought.

PREFACE

C. G. Jung was known all over the world as one of the pioneers of psychology and psychiatry. Trained as a physician he came to see that the different forms of mental illness were not entities in themselves, with a distinctive psychology, but disturbances of the normal working of the mind. He approached the treatment of mental illness from this point of view.

Jung's work is of special interest to students of medicine; also it has stimulated thought in sociology, theology and in general literature, because it contains the potentiality of growth in many directions.

In the expectation that Jung's influence will spread, the main features of Analytical Psychology are here set out as they developed.   E.A.B.

ACKNOWLEDGMENTS

The author and publisher wish to thank the following for permission to quote from copyright material. Routledge & Kegan Paul Ltd., London, and Bollingen Foundation, New York, for permission to quote from *The Collected Works of C. G. Jung,* and from *The Origins and History of Consciousness,* by Erich Neumann; Aldus Books Ltd., London, and Doubleday & Co., New York, for permission to quote from *Man and His Symbols,* by C. G. Jung; Barrie & Rockliff, London, for permission to quote from *C. G. Jung,* by E. A. Bennet; William Collins Sons & Co., London, and Pantheon Books, New York, for permission to quote from *Memories, Dreams, Reflections,* by C. G. Jung; W. W. Norton & Co., New York, for permission to quote from *An Autobiographical Study,* by Sigmund Freud; Basic Books, New York, for permission to quote from *The Life and Works of Sigmund Freud,* by Ernest Jones.

WHAT JUNG
Really SAID

ABBREVIATIONS USED

C.W. *The Collected Works of C. G. Jung*, listed on p. 6.
  London: Routledge & Kegan Paul.
  Princeton, N.J.: Bollingen Foundation.

M.D.R. *Memories, Dreams, Reflections*, C. G. Jung.
  London: Collins and Routledge & Kegan Paul,
   1963.
  New York: Pantheon Books, 1963.

M.S. *Man and His Symbols*, C. G. Jung; M-L. von
  Franz; J. L. Henderson; Jolande Jacobi; Aniela
  Jaffé.
  London: Aldus Books, 1964.
  New York: Doubleday & Co.

Types *Psychological Types*, C. G. Jung.
  London: Kegan Paul, Trench, Trubner & Co.
  Ltd., 1933.
  New York: Pantheon Books, 1959.

C.G.J. *C. G. Jung*, E. A. Bennet.
  London: Barrie & Rockliff, 1961.

1

STAGES IN
JUNG'S CAREER

BASEL UNIVERSITY

Jung, born in 1875, lived in Switzerland all his life. His father, a protestant parson, was in charge of the church at the Rhine Fall near Schaffhausen. Later the family moved to Basel where Carl Gustav was at school until 1895 when he became a medical student at the University of Basel. As his final medical examinations approached he wanted to specialize but reviewed the possibilities without reaching a decision. Surgery attracted him but this was not practicable because it required expensive post-graduate study beyond his father's means. Jung had to earn an income as soon as possible, and it seemed likely that a post in a general hospital would be the first step in his medical career. However, matters developed differently. An apparently trivial event gave him a clear lead in an unexpected direction.

While still a student he was invited by the children of some relatives to join in the game of table-turning with which they were amusing themselves. One of the group, a girl of fifteen, went into a trance and instead of her usual colloquial Swiss German she talked freely in literary German. Usually shy and retiring, she became confident and dignified. Jung was amazed. He knew the girl quite well but he had never seen this side of her before. His companions were not in the least concerned by her talk and behaviour, nor were they even curious. They accepted the whole thing as a game. Not so Jung. He found the incident astonishing. Here was a somewhat peculiar, though not unintelligent girl of fifteen, who suddenly, in a trance, exhibited the bearing and conversation of an educated woman. He wanted to understand something so arresting, so different from anything he had seen before. That his parents and the others accepted as an explanation the fact that the girl was always highly strung amazed him. He set about the solution of this difficult question systematically by keeping a detailed diary of the séances, written after each session, and he drew up a careful account of the girl's personality and behaviour in the waking state. This record provided a mass of psychological problems which at that stage in his career he could not understand. In his search for information that might explain the girl's behaviour Jung explored in vain the extensive literature on spiritualism. His teachers at the university showed no interest in the girl's peculiarities and thought he was wasting his time in considering such nonsense. He did not accept their opinion, and extended his reading in "the wide domain of psychopathic inferiority" which included epilepsy, hysteria and neurasthenia, and where he found

articles on rare states of consciousness such as somnambu-
lism and pathological lying. Some of the material was
relevant, and he used it, with his detailed notes of the girl's
condition, as the basis for his medical degree thesis. This
was published in 1902 and it is included in the English
Edition of Jung's Collected Works with the title: *On the
Psychology and Pathology of so-called Occult Phenomena.*[2]
As a senior student Jung attended the routine and rather
uninspiring lectures on psychiatry and visited the mental
hospital where he saw a few patients afflicted with the
commoner forms of insanity. Psychiatry in those days was
"generally held in contempt", writes Jung. "No one really
knew anything about it, and there was no psychology
which regarded man as a whole and included his pathological variations in the total picture. The director was
locked up in the same institution with his patients, and
the institution was equally cut off, isolated on the out-
skirts of the city like an ancient lazaretto with its lepers.
No one liked looking in that direction. The doctors knew
almost as little as the layman and therefore shared his
feelings. Mental disease was a hopeless and fatal affair
which cast its shadow over psychiatry as well. The
psychiatrist was a strange figure in those days. . . ."[3]
Richard von Krafft-Ebing was the author of the text-
book on psychiatry then used by medical students in
Basel. When preparing for his finals Jung put off reading
it till the last moment. He was not interested in psychiatry
and had no opinion for or against it. He was surprised
when he read of the incomplete state of development in
psychiatry and that the textbooks expressed the subjective
point of view of an author. This was in contrast to textbooks on medicine and surgery where objective informa-

tion was available. Then he had never heard of "diseases of the personality". This was a new world of thought, and naturally it stirred up memories of the girl who had gone into a trance. Apathy vanished and he was thoroughly interested. Krafft-Ebing's words, said Jung, "caused me tremendous emotion. I was quite overwhelmed by a sudden sort of intuitive understanding. I would not have been able to formulate it clearly then, but I felt I had touched a focus. And then on the spot I made up my mind to become a psychiatrist . . . this moment had been the real origin of my career as a medical psychological scientist."[4]

Although the decision was made suddenly, it was the culmination of a series of unanswered questions in Jung's mind, some going back to childhood. Amongst early memories were several striking dreams which he never forgot. At the time they were taken for granted; but questions came to his mind later: what could such a dream mean? Had it any meaning? His family lived in the country before moving to Basel, and Jung heard many strange stories and experiences recounted by the country people. In some unexplained way they were in the same category as his observations about the girl who had behaved strangely in a trance, although there was no obvious link between them. When he pondered the passages from Krafft-Ebing's book, Jung felt certain that psychiatry could provide the key at least to some of these obscure happenings.

On passing his final examinations Jung was invited to go as Assistant to one of his own professors who had accepted an appointment at another university. This was a compliment and his fellow students were envious; but to the surprise of his teacher and the astonishment of his friends, he turned the opportunity down and announced that he had decided to make his career in psychiatry. This decision was final; he never looked back, and he never regretted it.

Jung's career in psychiatry began in December 1900 when he became an Assistant at the Burghölzli, the University teaching hospital in Zürich, under Professor Eugen Bleuler, a leading figure in European psychiatry. Research was the order of the day and Jung, under supervision, began a careful inquiry into the cause of dementia praecox—later called schizophrenia—the commonest form of mental illness. He learnt the technique of cutting, and examining microscopically, sections of brain tissue from schizophrenic patients who had died; for it seemed probable that some disturbance of the brain would reveal the clue he was seeking. He set about this new and fascinating work with enthusiasm. But his hopes were not realised; the study of innumerable specimens threw no light on the meaning or the origin of schizophrenia.

WORD ASSOCIATION EXPERIMENTS

Jung, still occupied in his study of schizophrenic patients, then turned to another type of research—the Word Association Test. This well-known psychological test had been adapted by Sir Francis Galton, a cousin of Charles Darwin, to differentiate types of intelligence. In design it was quite simple: the person being tested (the subject) was told that a series of words would be read aloud slowly, and he was to respond immediately, to each, with the first word that came into his head. With a stop-watch the examiner noted the reaction time, that is the time in seconds the subject took to reply, and this was recorded on a chart. Usually there were about one hundred words on the list. Galton introduced all sorts of refinements in obtaining the exact measurement of the reaction time, even recording small fractions of a second. All this made the application of the test highly complicated. Unfortunately the mass of information obtained turned out to be of little or no value in estimating the level of intelligence.

Jung introduced a simple, though important, modification in giving the test: when a delayed reaction occurred he asked the subject why he had hesitated before giving a reply. To his surprise he found that the delay had not been noticed and so no explanation was forthcoming. He knew there must be a reason for it, and by searching and specific questioning this was often elicited. In one instance the word *horse* was followed by a reaction time of over a minute. Close enquiry revealed an emotional story of a runaway horse, an accident, scenes of excitement and so on. All of this the patient had completely forgotten.

It became evident that the response to the test words was influenced by the subject's emotion, and that the test was useful as a pointer to hidden (unconscious) emotion. Constructed for one purpose—to estimate intellectual qualities, the study of mental association—the word association test proved of more value in another direction, namely it showed an effect brought about by unnoticed emotion. Yet Galton, and others who had used it on thousands of people, had paid no attention to the emotion behind the delayed reaction and had merely registered the delayed response as a failure to react.

Graphs were drawn by Jung and they showed a correlation between the emotion accompanying a particular word and the reaction time. From these results it was concluded that two features were significant: firstly the emotion produced, and, secondly, that the delayed reaction occurred automatically and in response to some unrecognised process. It was too soon to draw conclusions from these records or to judge their importance. Certainly the unknown delaying action, operating apart from the subject's conscious intention, required more observation.

COMPLEX FORMATION

In Zürich and elsewhere at that time the emphasis in psychology, and its applications in psychiatric work, was on consciousness. On this basis experimental research into the psychology of the word association test was conducted. Jung, however, was of opinion that something more than consciousness and the operation of will-power was involved. He introduced the term *feeling-toned complex*, later abbreviated to *complex*, for what he judged to be a grouping of ideas in the unconscious, characterised by a peculiar, perhaps painful, quality of feeling that brought about the delayed reaction time. Numerous test results justified this conclusion and the complex, with its associated features, such as emotional effects, and individual quality, became the central feature in Jung's system of thought. Originally his teaching, now called *Analytical Psychology*, was called *Complex Psychology*—the psychology of the complex. Jung's term *complex* was subsequently taken over by all so-called "schools" of psychology, including the Freudian (Psychoanalysis) and Adlerian (Individual Psychology). Since the term gained a wide currency in everyday conversation it appears in the Shorter Oxford English Dictionary as "Jung's term for a group of ideas associated with a particular subject".

Considering the simplicity of the word association test it was a surprise to him that patients who understood what they were asked to do gave an immediate response to most of the words and then, unexpectedly, there was a delay over some word. Why was it that the subject was usually unaware of his hesitation? Jung's answer is that the word had "struck" a *complex*. Either the contents of the complex were completely unconscious or relatively unconscious, that is, the subject might be conscious of them at one time but not at another. From this it was concluded that the complex was activated in one environment or emotional setting but not in another. For example, a candidate, questioned in an examination, might fail to produce the answer although he had known it earlier. This is because many ideas within the personal unconscious are only relatively unconscious; they can well be conscious in other circumstances and in a different emotional setting. When the unfortunate candidate leaves the examination and is with his friends, the emotional atmosphere is different and he may remember the answer at once. Many ideas are, as it were, more deeply unconscious, and remain unconscious regardless of the transient emotional setting.

Jung saw a similarity between the formation of complexes and the fragmentation or partial break-up of the personality, such as happens in a nervous break-down. In other words, the complex behaves like a partial personality: it operates on its own and often in a way diametrically opposed to our conscious wishes. It is generally taken for granted by those who know nothing of unconscious mental activity, that the complex has been invented or "imagined" by the patient. For some perverse reason he has brought it forward, and had he behaved sensibly, the complex would not exist at all. As against this prejudice Jung says: "It has now been firmly established that complexes possess a remarkable degree of autonomy, that organically unfounded, so called "imaginary" pains hurt just as much as legitimate ones, and that a phobia of illness has not the slightest inclination to disappear even if the patient himself, his doctor, and common speech-usage all unite in asseverating that it is nothing but 'imagination'."[5]

It is certainly exasperating to all concerned when, in defiance of common sense—his own included—an otherwise reasonable person is at the mercy of irrational fears or compulsions for which no explanation is evident. This occurs today just as it has always done and patients with neurosis would prefer "something definite", such as a broken leg, about which they could take practical action.

General interest was aroused in the association test because of its simplicity. It had the additional advantage of making a fairly accurate quantitative and qualitative evalution of the person's response to a certain situation. This was because by its form the test reproduces the psychological situation of the dialogue. When a stimulus word is used it is more than a word: it becomes a condensed action, as though the subject were in a certain situation and responding to it. Usually in a dialogue, question and answer are complementary. Not so in the association test where the subject is confronted with the isolated and therefore disconcerting and ambiguous stimulus word. He cannot frame his reply in a sentence without departing from the instruction that his reaction must be with a *single* word.

As the reaction disturbances were the main object of interest to Jung and his colleagues, these were kept under observation. It was found that facts were revealed and registered on the chart which would have been avoided in ordinary discussion, because in the test the words appeared suddenly, unpredictably. When delay occurred it would be observed and investigation would follow to discover its significance.

A corresponding situation often arises in a talk between two people: the discussion becomes halting, seems to go off the point and misses its real purpose. This is because activated complexes frustrate one or perhaps both people. Remarks and answers are given which are later forgotten or denied.

Both in German and in English the word *complex*, in its psychological sense, is in everyday use. "Everyone knows nowadays," writes Jung, "that people 'have complexes'. What is not so well known, though far more important theoretically, is that complexes *have us* . . . But even the soberest formulation of the phenomenology of complexes cannot get round the impressive fact of their autonomy, and the deeper one penetrates into their nature—I might almost say into their biology—the more clearly do they reveal their character as *splinter psyches*." [6] This means that the complex behaves on its own, like a "broken off" or separate part of the psyche (mind). It is important to know that the psyche can become dissociated in consequence of emotional disturbance. This means that one part of the mind operates independently and apart from the main stream of consciousness. More important still is to discover the nature of the emotional upset so that the reasons for it can be made conscious and so capable of being understood. Dissociation of this type is not the same as a "split personality" when the mind may be permanently impaired.

That the complexes appear regularly in our dreams is beyond question. Again and again an unrecognised, possibly nameless, person figures in a dream. This is a personification of a complex. That consciousness, with its power of suppression, is lulled makes it possible for these personifications to appear. They take many forms, welcome or unwelcome. Often there is regret that the dream is over, and with it the behaviour we should not "dream" of permitting in waking life. We may reflect, complacently, that we are not responsible for our dreams! Complexes may also be observed in certain forms of psychosis (severe mental illness) in the form of voices. Here the complex has become audible. Likewise, in hallucinations (perceptions not conforming with reality) the complex has become visible.

Jung was a firm believer in getting to know his patients and he spent hours talking to them in the wards, trying to find out what had led to their illness. To be told that someone had been diagnosed as suffering from, say, schizophrenia was meaningless. He wanted to learn why that person was ill in that particular way and not in some other way. Each patient must be studied as an individual. He believed that every part of the organism was likely to be involved in the illness, and that the sick person's body as well as his mind had to be examined. Very soon he was able to show—and he was one of the first clinicians to do so—that the influence of emotion can be demonstrated physiologically as well as psychologically. In recording the reply to each stimulus word in the word association test a simultaneous and separate record was made of the pulse rate, of the breathing, and of the reading of the psychogalvanometer. This instrument was constructed to record quantitative variations in the electrical conductivity of the skin known to accompany emotional changes. Holding an electrode in each hand the subject was placed in circuit with a galvanometer and the resulting galvanic response was attested graphically. Whenever a stimulus word hit on a complex, it was observed that the recordings showed corresponding effects: the reaction time was prolonged, the volume of breathing restricted, the pulse rate increased and the reading of the psychogalvanometer altered. Results of this type would cause no surprise today, for we are familiar with the nature of psychosomatic manifestations. It was a very different state of affairs in the early nineteen-hundreds when the psychological and physiological effects of emotion and unconscious influences usually went unnoticed. Jung was ahead of his time in observing, and in using the fact, that the body and mind are by no means separate organisms; and in demonstrating that the body and the mind did not function independently, as the philosopher Descartes (1596–1650) had asserted, and many others, since his time, have believed.

Having established by the word association experiment that something within the individual, of which he was unconscious, could interfere with his conscious intentions, Jung set out to discover how the grouping of ideas below the surface, the complex itself, came into existence. As we know, the complex resembled a neurosis, that is, a nervous break-down. How then was this unhappy occurrence to be explained? One theory, once widely held and still accepted by some, is that an evil spirit had entered into the person and brought about the illness. In the Anglican Church and in the Moslem religion there are methods of exorcism which are occasionally used to drive out these nefarious spirits. Janet, a distinguished French psychiatrist, contended that weakness of constitution led to the dissociation of consciousness observed in hysteria and other illnesses. Unfortunately it was never clear how the dissociation worked. Jung looked on Janet's theory as a description rather than an explanation; it did not for account the remarkable strength of the complex which operated despite will-power and common sense. Nevertheless an answer to the mystery of the complex was at hand.

FREUD AND JUNG MEET

Freud's theories concerning the unconscious were not widely known in the early years of this century and their importance was not appreciated even by those who had heard of his work. Jung had read Freud's *Interpretation of Dreams* some years earlier, and he knew that Freud had made notable discoveries in methods of treating patients with neurosis. He was particularly impressed by Freud's theory of repression. Its significance will be seen if we consider what happens when we are confronted by a problem: possible solutions may be examined and a decision reached by reflection; alternatively the problem may be left unsolved, or—and this is the important step—unwittingly the conflict may drop out of consciousness because it has been repressed. Repression is an unnoticed, that is an unconscious, response to a conscious situation. Yet the conflict has not vanished; it remains active below the surface of consciousness and may, to our surprise and distress, produce symptoms. This, briefly, is Freud's theory of repression. Jung recognised that it gave a satisfactory explanation of the delayed reaction in the word association technique and of course he was tremendously interested. At once he wrote telling Freud that through the association test he had found experimental proof of the validity of his theory of repression and naturally Freud was pleased to have this confirmation of his theory, although he had not doubted its soundness. Jung was the first, probably the only, person to provide such proof. In writing Jung referred to the autonomous nature of the complex. Freud noted this, although he appeared not to have made use of this particular concept.

It is sometimes thought that Jung took up psychiatry under the influence of Freud. This is not the case. Having become interested in psychiatry through Krafft-Ebing, he began his formal training in December 1900 when he joined the staff of the Burghölzli Hospital. He writes: "I did not start from Freud, but from Eugen Bleuler and Pierre Janet, who were my immediate teachers. When I took up the cudgels for Freud in public, I already had a scientific position that was widely known on account of my association experiments, conducted independently of Freud, and the theory of complexes based upon them. My collaboration [with Freud] was qualified by an objection in principle to the sexual theory, and it lasted up to the time when Freud identified in principle his sexual theory with his method."[7]

Jung and his wife accepted Freud's invitation to visit

him in Vienna in 1907 and they received a cordial welcome. Earlier there had been correspondence between Freud and the so-called Zürich school of which Eugen Bleuler and Jung were the leaders, and this visit put matters on a personal basis. Writing of the interest shown in the psychiatrists from Zürich, Ernest Jones says: "It was natural that Freud should make much of his new Swiss adherents, his first foreign ones, and incidentally, his first Gentile ones. After so many years of being cold-shouldered, ridiculed and abused it would have needed an exceptionally philosophical disposition not to have been elated when well-known University teachers from a famous Psychiatric Clinic abroad appeared on the scene in whole-hearted support of his work." Jones also quotes a letter from Freud concerning Jung's association with the psycho-analytical movement: "His [Jung's] adherence is therefore all the more valuable. I was almost going to say it was only his emergence on the scene that has removed from psychoanalysis the danger of becoming a Jewish national affair."[8]

It was through the publication in 1906 of *The Psychology of Dementia Praecox* that Jung came to know Freud. In the Foreword to this book we read: "Even a superficial glance at my work will show how much I am indebted to the brilliant discoveries of Freud . . . Fairness to Freud, however, does not imply, as many fear, unqualified submission to a dogma; one can very well maintain an independent judgment. If I, for instance, acknowledge the complex mechanisms of dreams and hysteria, this does not mean that I attribute to the infantile sexual trauma the exclusive importance that Freud apparently does."[9]

For Jung the meeting was a mixture of expectation and disappointment. He hoped for much but seemed unable to get beyond what he regarded as the confines of Freud's narrow approach, his restricted perspective and concentration on tiny details, and his theoretical assumptions. Their initial conversation was very protracted. "Our first meeting," said Jung, "lasted for thirteen uninterrupted hours. We talked and talked and talked. It was a *tour d'horizon* in which I tried to make out Freud's peculiar mentality. He was a pretty strange phenomenon to me then, as he was to everybody in those days, and then I saw very clearly what his point of view was, and I also caught some glimpses already where I wouldn't join in."[10] Yet Freud made a great impression on Jung. In a later book we read: "Freud was the first man of real importance I had encountered; in my experience up to that time, no one else could compare with him. There was nothing in the least trivial in his attitude. I found him extremely intelligent, shrewd, and altogether remarkable. And yet my first impressions of him remained somewhat tangled; I could not make him out."[11]

2

PSYCHOLOGICAL TYPES

FREUD AND JUNG: AN INTERCHANGE OF IDEAS

Jung's appreciation of Freud's intellectual gifts and the nature of the work he was doing, and had done, counterbalanced to some degree his disappointment at Freud's insistence on the central importance of infantile sexuality. Although he could not support this, he did accept many of Freud's ideas and felt that his psychoanalysis was capable of development; so he was happy to be associated with him and their co-operation continued for over six years. During the whole of this time Jung was living in Zürich, and for years he was on the staff of the Burghölzli Hospital. Freud visited him and stayed at his house in Küsnacht-Zürich, and likewise Jung was Freud's guest in Vienna. Had they been living in the same town close co-operation might have been possible; but they had to be content with correspondence, occasional visits and meeting at conferences. Freud thought highly of Jung and took every opportunity of getting his opinion on future developments in the psychoanalytical movement. As the two pioneers met infrequently, they kept in touch by letter. Freud wrote to Jung every week. Jung found it difficult to answer all the letters. Freud expected replies and if none came he was in the habit of sending a telegram asking why.

Medical education in the early days of this century did not include systematic teaching on mental disorders, and few doctors knew anything about the subject. Freud was a notable exception and his writings showed original thinking on the psychology of the neuroses. Yet his emphasis upon infantile sexuality, in Jung's opinion, led him to neglect matters of equal or greater importance. He writes: "Freud's attitude towards the spirit seemed to me highly questionable. Wherever, in a person or in a work of art, an expression of spirituality (in the intellectual, not the supernatural sense) came to light, he suspected it, and insinuated that it was repressed sexuality. Anything that could not be directly interpreted as sexuality he referred to as 'psychosexuality'."[12]

Thus there were hints, long before the break came, that a separation was likely. Jung got the impression that Freud was determined to build up a complete system of psychological thought and so create an authoritative body of knowledge as a safeguard against disruption of his original work. Freud's personal experience had made it painfully obvious that his medical neighbours in Vienna, and in the wider world beyond, were not prepared to consider his claims. Amongst medical men there has always been resistance to change in established methods of treatment, especially in the treatment of mental illness. Amongst doctors and laymen mental illness is rather dreaded, and always has been, as though there was something dangerous or threatening about it; when emotions are aroused common sense is of little avail. That was why Freud determined to establish his work on a basis that could not easily be put aside by prejudiced opponents. After some years of solitary work he formed a small circle of colleagues on whose loyalty and co-operation he could rely. Within this group he was the unquestioned leader; opposition to his views disturbed him and it became obvious to all that critical comments were not welcomed. Jung recalls a conversation with Freud in Vienna, in 1910, which illustrates this: " 'My dear Jung, promise me never to abandon the sexual theory. That is the most essential thing of all. You see, we must make a dogma of it, an unshakable bulwark'. . . . In some astonishment I asked him, 'A bulwark—against what?' To which he replied, 'Against the black tide of mud'— and here he hesitated for a moment, then added 'of occultism.' . . . the words 'bulwark' and 'dogma' alarmed me: for a dogma, that is to say an indisputable confession of faith, is set up only when the aim is to suppress doubts once and for all . . . I knew I would never be able to accept such an attitude. What Freud seemed to mean by 'occultism' was virtually everything that philosophy and religion . . . had learned about the psyche."[13]

Freud wanted his system to be explicit, unequivocal, and Jung found this restraint distasteful: knowledge of the mind was limited and there was every reason to pursue research; this would be possible only if we remained open to change and to new ideas. Freud's desire for a firm foundation seemed likely to clog rather than facilitate advance; anything savouring of a preconceived theory would inevitably hinder development. Jung was all for extension, no limit must be imposed. Eventually the separation came because Jung failed to convince Freud that his (Freud's) original work could be expanded. Jung had plenty of ideas of his own, and he had no interest in setting the pattern for a new science designed as though to last for all time.

THE PARTING OF THE WAYS

In *The Psychology of the Unconscious* (re-named *Symbols of Transformation* in the Collected Works), Jung advocated, for one thing, a wider use of the term *symbol*. For him *symbol* was "the best possible description, or formula, of a relatively unknown fact; a fact, however, which is none the less recognised or postulated as existing."[14]

Freud did not look on a symbol in this way, preferring to give it what has been called a material significance, that is, treating it as though it referred to actual objects or persons, and so ruling out any immaterial or abstract ideas. Thus the term *symbol* was used by Freud semiotically, as a sign (*sema* in Greek means sign) of something quite well known, although not consciously recognised. Jung's concept was altogether different: *symbol*, for him, indicated some unspecified or indeterminate thing, material or immaterial, of which we have no precise knowledge although we assume its existence. Any other use of *symbol* seemed to him unpardonable blindness; a refusal to see something observable in its effects although not capable of precise definition. For example, the national flag of a country expresses more than can be set down in simple language; it is of greater significance than a sign or an alternative expression for something which can be described in a few plain words; it involves complex shades of meaning and inference and often it arouses intense emotion leading to action. Jung comments on Freud's view: "Those conscious contents which give us a clue, as it were, to the unconscious backgrounds are by Freud incorrectly termed symbols. These are not true symbols . . . according to his teaching they have merely the rôle of signs or symptoms of the background processes. The true symbol differs essentially from this, and should be understood as the expression of an intuitive perception which can as yet neither be apprehended better, nor expressed differently."[15]

This may appear as hair-splitting. It is not so; there is an important difference between the two meanings of the term symbol. Symbolism, as the word had been used for centuries before Freud's time, implied similarity, a conscious comparison. To quote from Dalbiez: "Freud had completely modified the usual meaning of the word 'symbol'. Psycho-analytical symbolism constitutes the exact antithesis of ordinary symbolism . . . whereas the ordinary symbol implies no direct causal relation with what it symbolizes, the Freudian symbol is essentially and by definition an effect of what it symbolizes."[16] For Freud the so-called material symbol refers to objects or to persons and—so he claimed—any alteration in this might very well be an attempt to escape from the unpleasant conclusions exposed by an acceptance of material symbols. Freud had in mind the possibility that a patient undergoing analysis might consciously or unconsciously try to avoid certain conclusions because he thought them unbecoming, and the psychiatrist treating the patient might fall into the same trap. Such a mistake must be avoided at all costs. Jung, on the other hand, argued that Freud's connotation of *symbol* was tantamount to claiming it as a substitute for the real thing, and this narrowed the meaning of the symbol and inevitably led to misunderstandings about symbolism and consequently misunderstandings about human psychology.

Moreover, Freud insisted that the symbol was a distorted expression of the inner, unconscious thoughts so that they appeared in consciousness with less emotional charge than the thing symbolized. Thus a knife, a stick, etc. may symbolize the penis. Symbols, in his view, were created out of the experience and environment of the individual. When this is compared with Jung's understanding of symbolism, it will be seen that he and Freud were at variance upon an important matter.

Jung's inability to accept Freud's view of symbols exposed him to criticism from Freud and others. His published opinion on the subject was backed by serious argument, and it came as a shock to Jung that Freud should reject what seemed to be a reasonable and significant development, even though this rejection came as no surprise. "I knew in advance that its publication would cost me my friendship with Freud for he would never be able to accept my views." This is exactly what happened. Jung's argument was that the concept of the Oedipus complex in Freud's teaching implied an incest tendency and that Freud in propounding his views on this complex "clung to the literal interpretation of it and could not grasp the spiritual significance of incest as a symbol."[17] His judgment of Freud's incest theory is set out in the last chapter (on *The Sacrifice*) of *Psychology of the Unconscious*. In the corresponding chapter of the same book, in its latest form entitled *Symbols of Transformation*,[18] Jung criticises Freud's emphasis on the importance of incest and womb-fantasies. Also he disputes Freud's belief that since the child's future character, temperament, and any neurosis that may appear, depends on the way in which it responds to, or deals with, the Oedipus complex (p. 48), the cause of every neurosis lies in the remote past. Jung's contention was that neurosis is caused by an inability to deal with a current problem and this state of mind may persist and be renewed day by day.[19]

Differences in outlook between Freud and Jung were becoming evident before they finally parted. Matters came to a head in 1912 at the Fourth Psychoanalytical Congress held in Munich. It would be idle to suppose that their disagreements were entirely on an academic level, for emotion often coloured the theoretical discussions. Jung had none of the qualities of a yes-man; he recognised Freud's qualities but he did not put him on a pedestal. There were many friendly arguments between the two in the early days of their association when Freud handed over responsibility to Jung for the further development of psychoanalysis. Yet emotion of a different order was only too plain when following a discussion with Jung—they were not alone—Freud fainted. Ernest Jones in his account of the episode records that Freud had fainted on a previous occasion after a discussion with Jung, and writes: "The occasion was, just as now, when Freud had won a little [verbal] victory over Jung."[20]

However, Jung's explanation seems more likely. During the lunch interval there was a general discussion about the action of an Egyptian king, Amenophis IV, in defacing his father's tomb. Freud maintained that such an act, by a son, was an example of a father complex. Jung said he did not agree and thought Freud's remark showed a misunderstanding or ignorance of Amenophis' action. "On the contrary," he said, "he [Amenophis] had held the memory of his father in honour, and his zeal for destruction had been directed only against the name of the god Amon which he had everywhere annihilated."[21] Amenophis' motives, he went on to explain, were to sweep away the numerous gods of Egypt and to replace them by a single god, the Sun. In his determined efforts to establish a monotheistic religion Amenophis had chiselled off many inscriptions in different parts of the country which incorporated the name of Amon, and these included that on his father's tomb. Jung writes: "Amenophis had been a creative and profoundly religious person whose acts could not be explained by personal resistances towards his father. . . . At that moment Freud slid off his chair in a faint . . . I picked him up, carried him into the next room and laid him on a sofa."[22]

It was at this Psychoanalytical Congress that Jung's *Psychology of the Unconscious*, and particularly the second part, came under fire. Freud could not accept Jung's views as a legitimate development of psychoanalysis. Yet in spite of Freud's expressed opinion, three-fifths of those at the conference voted in favour of Jung's re-election as President.[23]

It was the parting of the ways and Jung withdrew from the Freudian School. Freud himself, at a later date, when the dust of battle had long since settled, in speaking of Jung, remarked, "Jung was a great loss."

THE ORIGIN OF JUNG'S TYPOLOGY

A prolonged controversy, considerably tinged by emotion, blew up over the differences between Freud and Jung. Naturally this distressed Jung very much; yet in spite of his personal involvement he was the only person to realise that a difference of opinion, of such dimensions, must not be looked on merely as a personal disagreement on a specific issue. That two intelligent and sincere investigators were unable to agree on a matter of major importance was in itself an important psychological problem. To reduce it to the level of deciding that Freud was right and Jung wrong or *vice versa*, was to simplify the matter to the point of absurdity. Jung had no interest in controversy as such; he was concerned with extending our incomplete knowledge of psychology and psychopathology. His association with Freud had exposed him to severe criticism. In 1907, when they met, Freud was looked on with suspicion by the majority of doctors and intelligent laymen, particularly those in Vienna (p. 38). Jung was not deterred by unpopularity; his aim was to understand the principles upon which his work rested. He criticised Freud's arguments, although he did not criticise him personally; he had always been aware of Freud's remarkable qualities.

He believed the dispute with Freud rested on essential differences in their assumptions. Assumptions are necessary and cannot be avoided. Yet there is a danger that assumptions or hypotheses, being self-evident to ourselves, may lead us to make statements of a general character—

for example about the nature of the mind—and to claim that these are "true", forgetting that we are still talking of hypotheses and not of "absolute" truths. We are entitled to give a detailed presentation of what we have observed subjectively, for we see things in accordance with our particular psychology. Possibly this will be accepted by others who think as we do. But those who see things from a different angle may disagree. Jung writes: "What Freud had to say about sexuality, infantile pleasure, and their conflict with the 'reality principle', . . . can be taken as the truest expression of his personal psychology. It is the successful formulation of what he himself subjectively observed . . . Freud began by taking sexuality as the only psychic driving force, and only after my break with him did he take other factors into account. . . . For my part I have summed up the various psychic drives or forces . . . under the concept of energy . . . I do not mean to deny the importance of sexuality in psychic life, though Freud stubbornly maintains that I do deny it. What I seek is to set bounds to the rampant terminology of sex which vitiates all discussion of the human psyche, and to put sexuality itself in its proper place. Common sense will always return to the fact that sexuality is only one of the biological instincts, only one of the psychophysiological functions, though one that is without doubt very far-reaching and important." In the treatment of patients Jung always preferred "to look at man in the light of what in him is healthy and sound and to free the sick man from just that kind of psychology which colours every page Freud has written."[24]

How then was the psychological problem of the Freud-Jung controversy to be approached? Jung knew that he could hardly be impartial in assessing his differences with Freud; inevitably his own point of view would prevail. However, he thought of another plan. While in Vienna, visiting Freud, he had met Dr. Alfred Adler, one of Freud's earliest followers. Subsequently Adler had heated discussions which finally ended in total disagreement with Freud. Attempts at reconciliation failed, and he and Freud parted company. It should be possible, thought Jung, to study the psychological features in the Freud-Adler dispute objectively, and this might throw light on his own rupture with Freud.

Jung's work on typology originated in his efforts to find an answer to the conflict between Freud and Adler. This was not merely a matter of judging two opinions. As in his own break with Freud, he knew that two entirely different points of view were in conflict.

Adler's theory of neurosis, that is the meaning of the symptoms in a break-down, was based on the power principle. Symptoms were an instrument to gain power over those in the environment, such as members of the family. Above all things the patient sought his own security and supremacy. His goal was to achieve a feeling of power within himself, in contrast to his sense of inadequacy or failure summed up in the term inferiority complex. Whether in fact he was or was not inferior, the patient felt inferior. That was why he tried to put himself in a superior, a secure position. In these circumstances the world was seen from his individual standpoint; at the same time he had an undefined apprehension of difficulties that might lie ahead which impelled him to seek various devices by which these could be overcome so that the feeling of personal security would be undisturbed.

Unquestionably there was truth in Adler's contention—
as far as it went. Adler himself made out a good case for
his system of psychology. He was an excellent lecturer and
he wrote clearly and convincingly.

On the other hand Freud, seeing neurosis from another
angle, rejected Adler's claims. He declared that the
symptoms of every neurosis, together with the character
and temperament of the person concerned, were derived,
in a direct line of causality, from the manner in which the
child coped with what was known as the Oedipus complex.
This repressed Oedipus constellation mentioned above
(p. 43) comprises a sexual attitude on the part of the
child towards the parent of the opposite sex, coupled
with a desire to displace the parent of the same sex.

Adler's and Freud's views were contrasting ways of
understanding a neurosis and so the choice of one or the
other inevitably determined the lines along which treatment would be given. Freud's theory meant recovering
the response of the patient, in infancy and later, to the
problem caused by significant figures (for example, the
father and mother) at critical stages in life. These figures,
being actual individuals, were seen as such by the child.
Adler, on the other hand, saw the neurosis as teleologically
orientated; that is, the neurosis had a purpose, an objective.
Treatment lay in showing the patient that his "style of
life" was controlled by his feeling of hesitation towards
the future, and his precautionary outlook on the problems
of daily life. His life was governed by a desire to avoid
failure; to put the responsibility upon someone else. This
had a restricting influence on every part of his life and
thought; if one never entered the race one could never be
defeated. When this life-plan was explained adequately

to the patient, the illness would clear up. Adler attached great importance to the quality of the explanation given, and believed that if the explanation was all it should be the patient would see its significance, abandon his symptoms, and get well.

Jung's plan for studying the difference between Adler and Freud was to take each theory and show how it could be applied in understanding and interpreting the symptoms of an actual case of neurosis. This investigation, or rather comparative study, was carried out in considerable detail. Two conclusions emerged: that the theories were incompatible and, secondly, that there was a great deal to be said for both. Each theory, so far as Jung could discover, explained the psychology and psychopathology (abnormal psychology) of the case-history under investigation. If Jung's deduction is correct it would seem that a neurosis can be understood in two opposing ways, one the Adlerian, the other the Freudian. In other words, each investigator sees only one aspect of the patient and his illness, and insists that this, and this alone, is correct, and any other explanation is mistaken. This could not be right, thought Jung, for each theory contains sound observations explaining certain aspects of the neurosis, and although these may be incompatible, this does not make them mutually exclusive. It could safely be assumed that Adler and Freud, each practising in Vienna, were seeing the same sort of patients, that is, patients with neuroses. Jung concluded: "Each investigator most readily sees that factor in the neurosis which corresponds to his peculiarity . . . each sees things from a different angle, and thus they evolve fundamentally different views and theories. . . . This difference can hardly be anything else but a difference of temperament, a contrast between two different types of human mentality, one of which finds the determining agency pre-eminently in the subject, and the other in the object. . . . The spectacle of this dilemma made me ponder the question are there at least two different human types, one of them more interested in the object, the other more interested in himself? . . . I have . . . finally, on the basis of numerous observations and experiences, come to postulate two fundamental attitudes, namely introversion and extraversion."[25]

INTROVERTS AND EXTRAVERTS

In its simplest terms Jung concluded that Freud and Adler were of different types: Freud was an extravert, Adler an introvert. Events external to himself are all-important for the extravert and influence his life from birth onwards. Assuming Jung's assessment to be sound, we can understand that in Freud's psychoanalytical system special importance must be given to the behaviour of the parents and the child's reaction thereto. Likewise the supreme importance attributed by Freud to the grouping of ideas in the Oedipus complex, its repression, and the consequences that flow from this, become comprehensible if we accept the conclusion that Freud was an extravert.

Adler, in contrast, was an introvert. For the introvert the subjective response to circumstance is characteristic. What events mean for him is his first concern, and so he does not respond to them with the readiness of the extravert. Adler's *Individual Psychology* has a central theme: every psychical process must be understood as a personal preparation to attain a goal of superiority and thus displace the feeling of inferiority. According to Adler the child starts life with a feeling of inferiority, a distrust in its relation to its parents and to the world at large. In infancy, in childhood, during adolescence and as an adult, the individual devises plans to overcome this feeling of inferiority and to attain his superiority-goal.

Jung was not concerned with the details of Adler's psychology but with the central idea that the completeness of the personality, the power of the ego, must be preserved at all costs. It must triumph, or feel it has done so, over the unfavourable conditions of life.

Jung believed extraverts and introverts to be normal, healthy members of the community, constitutionally disposed to see life differently. This disposition is not fixed as a destiny; it can alter, or at any rate become less marked. Adler himself, by constitution an introvert, as witnessed by his system of thought, nevertheless seemed to alter as he got older, and his life-pattern appeared more extraverted than introverted. Introversion is often confused with introspection and this is thought to be an unhealthy state of mind. At times introspection is unhealthy; but it would be foolish to conclude that all reflection falls in this category. This would be an over-statement. To reflect, to ponder, to think, to look before we leap, is perfectly healthy. It is in this sense that Jung's term introversion should be understood. He believed that it was profitable and desirable to "look within". One reason why "introversion" is misunderstood comes from the prefix *intro*, an adverb of direction, for this may imply that the introvert's interest never gets beyond himself. Certainly this would be unhealthy. Jung drew attention to the easily observed fact that some persons, described as introverts, are aware that *they* are moved by their reflection upon an external object, while others, the extraverts, attribute the change in themselves to the object, something outside themselves affecting them.

Jung considered his own point of view very carefully—into which group did he fall? There was only one possible answer to this: he was an introvert. Yet Adler also was an introvert and he knew that he and Adler were very different. He thought Adler's outlook too narrow, and that his argument was determined mainly by the notion of power—power over others, power over the challenge of life. Jung had a wider outlook and rejected any rigid description or dogma, in terms of which personality might be explained. Eventually he came to the conclusion—which may seem obvious against the background of present-day knowledge—that there were variations among introverts (like Adler and himself), as there were among extraverts. Human nature with all its complexity could hardly be divided into two groups.

Jung never wavered about the value of his type-theory. But something had been lacking: he had tried to explain a highly complicated subject in too simple a way. For this reason he withheld the publication of his work for ten years.

Jung's book on *Psychological Types* appeared in 1920, but for years before this he had been concerned with the problem of types. He mentioned it in an essay published in 1916: ". . . there are personal types, variously orientated, whose mentality we ought never to try to constrain to the point of view proper to our own type. It is hard enough for one type completely to understand another type, but the perfect comprehension of another individual is quite impossible."[26] This was because such comprehension

stand a certain form of psychic activity that remains theoretically the same in varying circumstances. From the energic standpoint a function is a phenomenal form of libido, psychic energy, which theoretically remains constant, in much the same way as physical force can be considered as the form or momentary manifestation of physical energy."[30]

It will be apparent that Jung's typology, so simple to begin with, is now becoming complicated. We should not take very seriously the magazine-game of putting people into neat groups of extraverts and introverts. Extraversion and introversion, as two general attitude types, are each sub-divided with a four-fold classification of the functions of thinking, feeling, sensation and intuition. This makes eight variants, namely thinking, feeling, sensation and intuition in extraverted or introverted form. According to Jung's experience there were four, and only four functions. He had no bias in favour of the number four but there were no more than this or at all events he could not discern more. By thinking we are able to recognise the meaning or purpose of the object we observe, that is, we form a concept of it; feeling informs us of the value, to us, of the object; sensation relates to what is established by our senses of sight, touch, etc., and intuition brings in the idea of time as it points to possibilities that lie ahead. With this typological compass—a simile mentioned by Jung—it is possible to make an attempt to find our way within the far from simple psychological make-up of the average human being. Going further, the typology enables us to study human psychology in a more exact, more critical manner.

There are many other typologies. One of the earliest,

that of the Greeks, described human beings according to the state of the bodily humours or fluids: sanguine (blood); choleric (bile); phlegmatic (phlegm); melancholic (black bile). This famous typology, so difficult to explain physiologically, was widely accepted from the days of ancient Greek medicine up to the Middle Ages. Even now it is used conversationally when we speak of the sanguine, choleric, phlegmatic or melancholic person.

Kretschmer, a German psychiatrist, associated the qualities of physical build with significant features in the personality. His typology, published later than Jung's, has similarities to it, but many differences. Prominent amongst these is that Kretschmer deals with abnormal personalities and Jung with normal. Kretschmer's schizoid would correspond to a pathological example of Jung's introverted type, and his cycloid to a pathological example of Jung's extraverted type.

Jung's typology omits any reference to bodily characteristics and is confined to the classification of normal psychic data. This should be noted, for Jung considered the symptoms of neurosis and psychosis (with certain exceptions such as those caused by infections or injury) as disturbed normal processes, something that intruded upon the harmonious life of the individual. Unlike the Greeks and others, he makes no claim that his typology is complete or that it is the best possible typology.

When *Psychological Types* was published in English its translator, the late Dr. H. G. Baynes, described it as Jung's crowning work. It was a detailed exposition of the psychology of consciousness, and so seemed to complete Jung's already well known work on the psychology of the unconscious. This included *The Psychology of Dementia Praecox, The Psychology of the Unconscious*, and a few papers, including one *On the Importance of the Unconscious in Psychopathology*, read at the Annual Meeting of the British Medical Association at Aberdeen in 1914. "Crowning work" strikes a premature note of finality for Jung's contributions to psychological thought continued up to 1961, the year of his death.

Consciousness is the relation of psychical facts to a fact called the ego, and nothing can be conscious without an ego to which it refers. A baby has no awareness of an ego and its mother and others appear to be taken for granted as though identical with itself. In infancy and childhood consciousness of an ego gradually develops and usually from the age of eight or nine onwards the child realises "I am". Hence Jung speaks of consciousness as derived from the unconscious. In *Psychological Types* the hypothesis of the unconscious is implicit. There is an inevitable correlation between the unconscious and the conscious manifestation of extraversion, introversion, and each of the four basic functions. What is notably absent in consciousness will be found in the unconscious. This is of considerable practical importance in psychotherapy where a chief aim is to make conscious (and so controllable) repressed or forgotten memories, and thus restore healthy, or at any rate healthier, functioning.

3

UNCONSCIOUS

MENTAL ACTIVITY

THE PSYCHOGENESIS OF MENTAL ILLNESS

Some years before his medical studies began Jung became interested in philosophy and particularly in Kant's *Critique of Pure Reason* and the writings of Schopenhauer, Carus, von Hartmann and others. He was aware that the unconscious psyche had existed for centuries as a postulate in philosophic thought. His own first glimpse of the fact that there was another world—the unconscious of later times—came when he observed the mediumistic girl mentioned earlier (p. 22). He felt this other world had a life of its own, quite apart from the life of consciousness. But he was unable to understand what it might be. That he could not understand it did not detract from its importance; many things exist apart from our under-

standing, and Jung felt no urge to reject every notion he
was unable to prove: their existence did not depend on
proof. An experience continues to exist apart altogether
from our ability to explain it. Jung knew very well the
difficulty many had in thinking of the psyche, the mind,
as anything but a personal possession. This was because
they had no experience of the unconscious and looked on
a dream, for instance, as "only" a dream, as if it had no
life of its own. This was not a problem for him. He had
observed the mediumistic girl and this had given him the
idea of the psyche as an objective phenomenon with its
autonomous laws. How remarkable it was that this girl
of fifteen could behave, in her trance, like a woman of
thirty, as if seeing her life ahead. These personal reflections were most important for Jung. So, of course, was his
knowledge that philosophers had written of the unconscious; but their work had an abstract quality, it lacked
immediacy.

Without doubt these early reflections made Jung all
the more appreciative of Freud's work on dreams when he
came to know it. His indebtedness to Freud is unqualified. "By his evaluation of dreams he discovered an
avenue to the unconscious which had hitherto existed only
as a philosophical postulate."[31] Here was a tool that had
seemed irretrievably lost since the earliest attempts to
read the message of dreams.

Jung's research in the Burghölzli Hospital amongst
disturbed and chronic patients was stimulated by a
determination to find out what illness of this type could
mean. It seemed unrelated to the diseases of general
medicine. He was not prepared to accept terms, such as
schizophrenia, as though the name itself meant some-

thing; he wanted to know what lay behind the bizarre symptoms of the schizophrenic. Possibly it was some complicated human problem; possibly a mixture of physical and mental illness. As well as personal experiences, his word association experiment (Chapter 1) convinced Jung that unconscious mental activity was a reality. In many instances, he felt sure, the illness had been brought on by unrecognised mental conflict. Of course this conclusion could not be proved, but it was strongly suggested by his experience in talking to the patients. His surmises about the influence of the unconscious upon his patients were a real stimulus in his work and he pursued his investigation with enthusiasm.

Jung's interest in the cause and treatment of schizophrenia, aroused by nine years work in the Burghölzli Hospital, continued all his life. Yet the solution eluded him. Some of his schizophrenic patients became chronic invalids; some got better, and yet the reason for the improvement was unknown and so treatment was speculative and the enigma of schizophrenia remained.

In 1919 Jung read a paper before the Section of Psychiatry, Royal Society of Medicine, London, entitled *On the Problem of Psychogenesis in Mental Disease.*[32] (Psychogenesis means originating in the mind.) Twenty years later he read a second paper before the same body *On the Psychogenesis of Schizophrenia.*[33] He was still convinced that psychogenesis was important, but he left open the possibility that other influences were at work. Psychogenesis did not mean an exclusively psychological origin. There remained the question: was the illness the result of a primary weakness of the ego, that is of consciousness, or due to an inordinate strength of the unconscious? As recently as 1956, in a broadcast in thirty languages by the Voice of America, Jung spoke on "Recent Thoughts on Schizophrenia". This talk was reproduced and translated into German in 1959 and is now available in English.[34] Dealing with the problems that have still to be answered about schizophrenia, Jung believed the wise course was to advance a speculative hypothesis, based on facts known to us, and on our deductions from the observation and treatment of patients. Although our knowledge of the psychology of schizophrenia is incomplete, it seems likely that some features in the mental life of the schizophrenic go beyond a personalistic explanation. There is a disturbance of the normal capacity to build up ideas, an inability to use the capacity for feeling, and emotional values appear to be grossly upset or absent. In a neurosis personalistic contents may be explained by biographical data; but in the schizophrenic, collective elements, *archetypal* structures, are found and a personalistic causality fails to explain their peculiar archaic form and meaning. Jung adds: ". . . no specifically psychological processes which would account for the schizophrenic effect, that is, for the specific dissociation, have yet been discovered. I have come to the conclusion that there might be a *toxic cause* traceable to an organic and local disintegration, a physiological alteration due to the pressure of emotion exceeding the capacity of the brain cells."[35]

Whether or not there is a toxin is a subject for physiological research. Likewise, an equally important question awaits an answer from psychopathologists: what meaning can be found for the *contents* of schizophrenic thought processes?

Two terms have been used above which must now be explained: (a) unconscious mental activity, and (b) personal and collective unconscious.

UNCONSCIOUS MENTAL ACTIVITY

Towards the end of the last century F. W. H. Myers, author of *Human Personality and its survival of Bodily Death* (1903) and other investigators of spiritualistic phenomena, such as automatism, possession and ecstasy, spoke of mental activity beyond the margin of the conscious field. Words such as the subliminal self, the subconscious, the unconscious, were well-known outside philosophic circles before Freud's day. So too were the phenomena of the hypnotic trance. When Freud, investigating the nature of dreams, opened up a road to the unconscious (p. 59), his conclusions were received with cool reserve, for doctors looked on spiritualists and hypnotists as charlatans and they were disposed to put Freud in the same category.

Freud's theory of repression (p. 33) was for Jung a sound explanation of why the unconscious had become unconscious: a conscious experience proving unacceptable and causing conflict, was repressed and so became unconscious. Had there been no repression the experience would have remained conscious; hence the unconscious, composed as it is of repressed material, was of the same quality as consciousness. This repressed material, being unconscious (i.e. unknown to consciousness), is only available indirectly through understanding dreams, discovering the meaning of symptoms or revealing the significance of complexes.

It is sometimes thought that the unconscious with its

numerous subtle and obscure manifestations must be abnormal, and therefore that the unconscious is absent in normal people. This mistaken idea was a source of anxiety to some of Jung's patients. An exaggeration of the process of thought customary in an individual can become abnormal. Should the exaggeration be excessive, and especially if it leads to unusual actions, it should be considered abnormal and treated accordingly. So-called normal people often have transient hysterical or obsessional symptoms. These should not be regarded as evidence of a disordered mind. All available knowledge supports the view that the unconscious is a natural phenomenon. It contains many aspects of human nature—the dark and the light, the wise and the foolish, the beautiful and the ugly, the profound and the superficial. To be ignorant of the fact that we have an unconscious or to think that its contents can safely be put on one side, is to discard a part of our nature which can be of the highest importance in understanding human psychology, as well as in the treatment of illness.

It is interesting to observe that Freud in Vienna using psychoanalysis, and Jung in Zürich with the word association experiments, independently reached a similar conclusion on the origin of the complex: that it indicated activity within the unconscious. Jung was much impressed to observe that the unconscious mind acted autonomously, that is, independently of conscious motivation.

THE PERSONAL UNCONSCIOUS

As mentioned earlier (p. 40), the publication in 1912 of *The Psychology of the Unconscious* showed that Jung had widened the use of the term *symbol*, or rather, had given it its original connotation. From his investigation of the objective evidence of mental illness and of the symptoms mentioned by patients, Jung was convinced that not all of their unusual experiences could be explained on the basis of their personal history and the repression of ideas that conflicted with their accepted ideals. Mistaken judgments that cannot be corrected by explanation—that is delusions, or hallucinations, such as hearing voices—sometimes seemed to be outside any personal experience. Likewise the material in some dreams was utterly strange to the patient who had no idea what it might mean. But however bizarre these apparently impersonal experiences might be, they must have some meaning. With these two groups of ideas, some personal, others impersonal, Jung put forward the hypothesis that there is a general division of the unconscious into the *personal* and the *collective* (impersonal) unconscious, which, as the name implies, goes beyond personal experience.

The experiments in word association discussed earlier (p. 25) supported this hypothesis of personal and impersonal unconscious contents. It was noted, for instance, that when a stimulus-word happened to touch upon a topic related to a complex the reaction time was affected, and sometimes the response given surprised the subject. This latter was interpreted as an answer direct from the complex, for the complex behaves as a separate personality, acts autonomously and constantly interferes with our conscious intentions. It is as though the complex had a mental life of its own, a secondary or partial personality living unnoticed within us. When this complex was made conscious, as happens in psychological treatment, the secondary or partial personality disappears. In other words, the patient is relieved of that particular complex, whatever form it took. Supposing the patient had a fear of being shut up in a closed space, such as a small room or a railway carriage, the group of ideas forming the symptoms is the complex. It was because of repression that such complexes came into existence in the first instance.

THE COLLECTIVE UNCONSCIOUS

In addition to these, Jung held that there are contents of another order. They have never been in consciousness and so could not be the result of repression, which is a personal matter. They are impersonal, or collective. Jung had noted these contents of the mind again and again and put forward the hypothesis of the collective unconscious as a possible explanation. Such complexes "grow out of the unconscious and invade the conscious mind with their weird and unassailable convictions and impulses. . . . To my mind it is a fatal mistake to regard the human psyche as a purely personal affair and to explain it exclusively from a personal point of view. Such a mode of explanation is only applicable to the individual in his ordinary everyday occupations and relationships."[36]

With the hypothesis of a non-personal part of the mind Jung's teaching had become distinct from Freud's. Jung's "personal unconscious" covered Freud's concept of an unconscious composed of personal contents, derived from repression. This was valid as far as it went and Jung accepted it, but he supplemented it by the new concept— the collective unconscious. This term was, and is, often misunderstood. It has been confused with a group mind, that is the unconscious action of the crowd replacing conscious individual activity. Nothing of this sort was in

Jung's mind. Unlike the personal unconscious, the collective unconscious is not a personal acquisition. However unique each mind may seem to be, it has much that is indistinguishable from other minds because all minds have a common substratum or foundation. This Jung calls the collective unconscious.

ARCHETYPE AND INSTINCT

A feature in the collective unconscious is its origin in heredity—unlike the personal unconscious which comes from individual experience. So far as we know the personal unconscious consists for the most part of *complexes*, the collective unconscious is made up of *archetypes*, that is, pre-existent forms or original forms. Jung held that "the instincts [inborn, unlearned tendencies] form very close analogies to the archetypes—so close, in fact, that there is good reason for supposing that the archetypes are the unconscious images of the instincts themselves; in other words, they are *patterns of instinctual behaviour*. The hypothesis of the collective unconscious is, therefore, no more daring than to assume there are instincts."[37]

Jung laid considerable emphasis upon the universal character of the collective unconscious: ". . . it has contents that are more or less the same everywhere and in all individuals. It is, in other words, identical in all men and thus constitutes a common psychic substrate of a suprapersonal nature which is present in every one of us."[38]

The late Professor Henri Frankfort[39] criticized Jung's hypothesis of the collective unconscious, and particularly its claim to universal validity. He writes: "For him [Jung] the unconscious is never fully understood, never a surveyable part of the human self, the origin of creative ideas. While in Freud's explanation the images emerging from the unconscious are circumscribed by the experiences of the individual person, Jung asserts that these images never represent more than part of the material and that moreover in certain circumstances symbols and figures can turn up with which the historian of religion is familiar, but not the patient, for whom—that is to say, for whose consciousness—they have no significance. . . . Jung has called these—allegedly suprapersonal—images and figures archetypes, and their totality the collective unconscious." Frankfort argues that historical observations have taught us "that the archetypes are by no means universal." As an example he cites the feeling of a child towards father and mother, which he claims is "strongly influenced by the social structure. In a matriarchal society where the father is, as it were, a stranger—or even a visitor—in the mother's house and the maternal uncle is head of the family, filial emotions are different from those in a patriarchal polygamous society, and they are different again in a patriarchal monogamy."

This argument seems to imply that Jung claimed universal identity in the manifestations of the various archetypes seen in typically human situations such as the relation of a child to its father and mother, or to either. Professor Frankfort points out that dissimilarities in social structure are very common. But a child would not be expected to distinguish his actual father from another acting *in loco parentis*. The relation with such a person would be of a like kind in every child, whatever the social structure. Frankfort has other observations on Jung's concept of the archetypes and his scholarly essay provides the type of criticism Jung would have welcomed. That Frankfort recognised his calibre is clear: ". . . the real point of his [Jung's] discoveries is that they deal with the realities of the living psyche, the working of the imagination, and the symbols and figures welling from the unconscious mind in dreams. The connections which Jung has uncovered between these happenings and the strivings, hopes and anxieties—in short with the inner life—of the dreamer have an impressive width and depth."

Jung was always opposed to any claim of an absolute nature and believed that we were only at the beginning of what may in the future be learnt of human psychology. Students at times are puzzled because his claims concerning archetypes appear too comprehensive. Had they known him they would have understood that he was always open to learn, always ready to abandon a hypothesis if good reasoning demanded the change. Jung had the mind of an explorer: he felt there was more beyond; that our maps would be re-drawn again and again. This open-mindedness, however, did not require him to abandon what he had discovered, particularly as no alternative explanation to account for what he had termed archetypes was forthcoming from those who questioned the value of his hypothesis. If certain themes associated with ancient mythological material appeared in the dreams of a patient Jung accepted this as a fact and pointed out the parallel to his patient. Such material would probably be applicable also to other patients, and he constantly found this to be true. He never insisted that such parallels indicated the certainty of an identical inheritance in human beings the world over. Sometimes it seemed likely, sometimes unlikely, that this would be the case. A race with an ancient cultural heritage, in Jung's opinion, had a collective experience not available to other races. All the same, in the minds as in the bodies, of each, similarities would be expected.

Jung did not coin the word *archetype*. It has been in use for centuries and means the original pattern or proto-type from which copies are made. Thus in Plato's theory of "ideas" or "forms", a particular horse, for instance, would share a quality found in all horses. Thus the collective idea or form is the antithesis of the individual because it is peculiar to a group of individuals rather than the property of only one. So the collective unconscious is not a personal possession or acquisition, but universal. As the instincts, the unlearned motives, are an inborn manner of acting, so the archetypes supply an inborn manner of comprehension. Jung writes: "The hypothesis of a collective unconscious belongs to the class of ideas that people at first find strange but soon come to possess and use as familiar conceptions . . . *Archetype* is apposite and helpful, because it tells us that so far as the collective unconscious contents are concerned we are dealing with archaic or—I would say—primordial types, that is with universal images that have existed since the remotest times."[40]

In discussing his views on the collective unconscious Jung often compared the history of the mind with that of the body. Human bodies have a distinct anatomical conformity throughout the world. In spite of a varied history with extremes of temperature and differing habits of life and custom, human bodies, with only minor differences, remain much the same. So also with the mind. It too has a basic conformity and Jung felt convinced that extended studies, particularly in dream psychology, would lead to discoveries in the development and structure of the mind on a par with those made in comparative anatomy.

No loss of individuality follows from the concept of the collective unconscious. Instincts have a personal manifestation, and are accepted as our personal property; no one would think of them otherwise. That instincts are common to the race does not eliminate a personal sense of ownership in our own instincts. Likewise the collective unconscious is experienced personally.

Jung sometimes used *objective psyche* as synonymous with *collective unconscious*; but he preferred the older term. He thought of his work on the collective unconscious as his most important contribution to psychology. When asked about his personal myth—that which gave a meaning to life—he replied immediately, "Oh, that is the collective unconscious."

Seeing that *heredity* has been mentioned in connection with the hypothesis of the collective unconscious, some have assumed that archetypes and acquired characteristics are the same. Jung was at pains to correct this misunderstanding. He held that the unconscious structure of the psyche is an inborn, *a priori* factor. Thus a new-born child is a complicated, but at the same time a sharply defined, individual entity. We cannot observe this directly until the first visible manifestations of psychic life appear. Their individual character is then seen beyond any shadow of doubt. In other words, we become aware of a unique personality behind them. A neutral observer, let alone the mother, would not question this. John Locke (1632–1704), the physician and philosopher, contended that the child's mind, at birth, is comparable to a plain sheet of wax upon which experience writes. No one agrees with this today. Jung's contention is opposed to Locke's. He found it impossible to believe that the details constituting the unique personality of the infant spring into being at the moment they appear. "We explain by heredity the gifts and talents traced back through generations . . . Likewise the reappearance of complicated instinctive actions in animals that have never set eyes on their parents and therefore could not possibly have been 'taught' by them. . . . The idea that 'the human quality' is not inherited but comes into being in every child anew would be just as preposterous as a primitive belief that the sun which rises in the morning is a different sun from that which set the evening before."[41]

THE HYPOTHESIS OF THE COLLECTIVE UNCONSCIOUS AND ITS ORIGIN

Dreams occupied an important place in Jung's life and often seemed to anticipate a new development in his work. Certainly a dream foreshadowed, or at all events gave an introduction to, his concept of the collective unconscious. This was during 1909 when Freud and Jung travelled together to and from the United States, having been invited to give a series of lectures. During the trip they analysed one another's dreams. Inevitably this involved a personal analysis which, by today's standards, might seem short. Dr. David Stafford-Clark suggests that this analysis never took place: "There is an amusing but almost certainly apocryphal tale about an attempt at mutual analysis between Freud and Jung which supposedly contributed to their ultimate disagreement and separation."[42] Dr. Stafford-Clark gives no evidence to account for his scepticism. Perhaps he assumed that Ernest Jones would have mentioned the analysis in his *Sigmund Freud* if it had taken place. That this mutual analysis did take place has been affirmed by Jung in print: "The trip to the United States which began in Bremen in 1909 lasted for seven weeks. We were together every day, and analysed each other's dreams."[43] Jung and others have referred to it in lectures, and Jung spoke of it in a B.B.C. broadcast, as well as in private. Details of their interviews were not given. Hitherto the accuracy of Jung's statement has not been questioned. Both Freud and Jung believed in analysis, and as Freud had personal difficulties he asked for Jung's help in clearing them up. This was widely known long before Jung died in 1961. Dr. Stafford-Clark could have made enquiries if he had any doubt about the accuracy of the "tale". To describe the mutual dream-analysis as he does is reminiscent of Ernest Jones' comments about Jung's relation with Freud in his *Sigmund Freud—Life and Work*.*[44] It should be remembered that for several years Freud held Jung in high esteem. On his own initiative he made him perpetual President of the Psychoanalytical Association with responsibility for the further development of psychoanalysis. It is difficult to see why it should be "amusing and almost certainly apochryphal" that Freud and Jung should analyse one another's dreams.

* In 1959 I asked Jung about the incidents mentioned by Ernest Jones, including the conversations at Bremen before Freud and Jung left on the American visit. He said that Jones' report was incorrect and added: "Jones never asked me about those early days and he could easily have done so. Jones was not there. Freud and Ferenczi were dead and I was the only person who could have given accurate information."—E.A.B.

In the course of their mutual analysis Jung had a dream and asked for Freud's observations on it. This is the dream:

"I was in *my* house. It was a big complicated house, vaguely like my uncle's very old house built upon the ancient city wall at Basel. I was on the first floor; it was nicely furnished, rather like my present study. The room was of the eighteenth-century type and the furniture very attractive. I noticed a fine staircase and decided I must see what was downstairs, and so I descended to the ground floor. Here the structure and fittings seemed of the sixteenth century or older. It was rather a dark room; the furniture was old and heavy and I thought to myself, this is very nice—I didn't know it was here. Perhaps there is a cellar beneath. And there was. It was of very ancient structure, perhaps Roman. I went down a dusty much-worn staircase and found bare walls with the plaster coming off, and behind were Roman bricks; there was a stone-flagged floor. I got an uncanny feeling going down the staircase with a lantern in my hand. I thought now I am at the bottom. But then in a corner I saw a square stone with a ring in it; this I lifted, and looked down into a lower cellar, which was very dark, like a cave or possibly a tomb. Some light came in as I lifted the stone. The cellar was filled with prehistoric pottery, bones and skulls. I was quite amazed and as the dust settled I felt I had made a great discovery. There the dream ended and I woke up."*

* Jung mentioned this dream to me in 1951 and in 1961 it was published.[45] Jung read this book in typescript and added his comments, including one or two verbal alterations. For instance, he added the words, "in *my* house" and remarked that this was of special importance because it showed that he felt identified with the house, it represented

Jung was puzzled by the dream; but he had some "hunches" about it. He recalled how he had watched Freud turning the dream over in his mind, and wondering what he would say. Freud concentrated on the bones and the skulls and disregarded the rest of the dream. He thought it meant that Jung was associated with someone whom he wanted to die—the skulls could only mean death. "Was there any such person?" asked Freud, and Jung replied, "No, not at all." But Freud pressed the point and Jung questioned him about his insistence on the dream's death-wish and asked him to whom he thought it would refer—would it be a particular person such as his wife? "Yes," said Freud, "it could be that—that's the most likely meaning." Jung was surprised and pointed out that there were several skulls, not just one. Yet Freud still concentrated on the features in the dream suggesting death. Jung asked, "What do you make of the other parts of the dream?" but Freud was not interested in them.

An impressive feature about the dream was the atmosphere of expectancy; it was like an exploration. Jung spent a good deal of time thinking about the dream, apart from the discussion with Freud. His reflections continued on and off for months—indeed for years after that. He was quite unable to account for the dream in personal terms. Then it occurred to him that the house might represent stages of culture, the different floors portraying different eras—as in excavation remnants of houses are found beneath the foundations of present-day buildings. With

the external aspect of the personality, the side seen by others. But in the dream the interior of the house was not familiar. An account of the dream was published again in 1963.[46] While the wording is not identical with the account just given, the meaning is the same.—E.A.B.

its varied construction, Jung thought the house in the dream might carry some historical allusion. Could the dream have a structure resembling that so often seen in human history? "It was then, at that moment," said Jung, "I got the idea of the collective unconscious."[47] It seemed a possible, even a significant hypothesis. The more Jung thought about it, the more satisfied he became that, schematically, the formation in layers seen in the dream might resemble the development of our own or of other cultures; that in addition to the personal features in the psyche there were impersonal or autonomous elements, some apparently timeless, others relating back through the ages.

For Jung one of the most arresting features about the collective unconscious was that thoughts and ideas, never before conscious, emanate spontaneously from this impersonal source. Experiences of this kind were numerous and disposed him to believe the unconscious to be more than a store-house of past experiences due to repression or forgetting. He writes: ". . . many artists, philosophers, and even scientists owe some of their best ideas to inspirations that appear suddenly from the unconscious. . . . We can find clear proof of this fact in the history of science itself. For example, the French mathematician Poincaré and the chemist Kekulé owed important scientific discoveries (as they themselves admit) to sudden pictorial 'revelations' from the unconscious. The so-called 'mystical' experience of the French philosopher Descartes involved a similar sudden revelation in which he saw in a flash the 'order of all sciences'. The British author, Robert Louis Stevenson, had spent years looking for a story that would fit his 'strong sense of man's

double being', when the plot of *Dr. Jekyll and Mr. Hyde*
was suddenly revealed to him in a dream." [48]

Jung's ideas about the collective unconscious appeared
in his *Psychology of the Unconscious* in 1912 and the book
also contained his statement upon the meaning of symbols
(p. 40). Freud himself in one of his latest books referred
to our "archaic heritage" and "memory traces" of former
generations. He acknowledged that his interest in anthropology was aroused by Jung: it was "the explicit indications
of Jung as to the far-reaching analogies between the
mental products of neurotics and of primitive peoples
which led me to turn my attention to the subject." [49]

JUNG'S EMPIRICAL OUTLOOK

When the notion of the unconscious was introduced to
psychology it had a cool reception, and it is not surprising
that the hypothesis of the collective unconscious was met
with chilly reserve. Jung himself was aware of the difficulty
in providing so-called scientific proof in support of the
concept, and that is why he speaks of it as a hypothesis
which gives an adequate or satisfactory explanation of
observable facts. "If I speak of the collective unconscious,
I don't assume it as a principle; I only give a name to the
totality of observable facts, i.e. archetypes. . . ." [50]

Since the hypothesis of the collective unconscious gave
a reasonable explanation of puzzling features in his clinical
work, Jung was naturally on the alert and keen to examine
every possible application of this theory.

Long before he had the dream of the mediaeval house
Jung had used dream-analysis in the treatment of patients.
He had to work out the meaning of the dreams with the
associations of the dreamer. A dream of flying in an

aeroplane that crashed would be meaningless without the associations; but with these the meaning could as a rule be worked out. Sometimes the dreamer could not say anything about the motifs in a dream, as happens regularly with children. When archetypal themes appear in children's dreams and fantasies there is little or no hope of getting associations for the child may have no ideas to offer. This is not surprising as the material cannot be derived from consciousness. Often a child mentions a dream on waking, or wakes in the night, speaks of a dream and goes to sleep again. In the morning it may have faded from memory. Dreams of this type are well known and their meaning may sometimes be worked out by a process of comparison with the dreams of other children or with mythological references. Here the analyst's experience and knowledge will be of value. Fairy tales are usually of archetypal material and they appeal to children because the child's mind at this stage of development is but little removed from the deeper, collective layers of the unconscious from which consciousness comes.

Jung noted a further source of archetypal material in the delusions of some schizophrenic patients he had observed in hospital. Often the content of these delusions was incomprehensible until he recognised similarities between the delusion and certain mythological and historical material. To his astonishment he found constantly that there was a parallelism. Such investigations into the delusions were not always successful, and then the delusion remained a mystery. Nevertheless the successes were encouraging. Their value lay in making the content of the illness comprehensible to Jung. Only by understanding the illness could he find a basis for treatment.

That Jung should rely on mythological parallels may surprise those who equate mythology with fictitious or supernatural stories. It is not as simple as this. Myths existed long before science and express life as it is seen and experienced more accurately than objective scientific assessment. Their importance is widely recognised. Thus Arnold J. Toynbee, trying to solve problems of the cultural inequality of various extant human societies, found the nineteenth-century would-be scientific impersonal explanations useless. He writes: "The breakdown of these . . . drove me to turn to mythology. I took this turning rather self-consciously and shamefacedly, as though it were a provocatively retrograde step. I might have been less diffident . . . if I had been acquainted at the time with the works of C. G. Jung, they would have given me the clue."[51]

While Jung's clinical work supported the hypothesis of the collective unconscious, it fell short of proof, as proof is understood in scientific work. Nevertheless, similarities called for some explanation. Now and then the content of a delusion contained archetypal motifs of which it seemed impossible the patient could have had knowledge. To give a concrete picture of "that deeper psychic activity" called the collective unconscious Jung has published extracts from the medical history of a delusional patient. At first he simply could not understand what the man was talking about. Later when the translation of an ancient papyrus was published, he was amazed to find that it contained material strikingly similar to the content of the patient's delusion.[52] It is, of course, open to any one to explain such material on the basis of another hypothesis; but until this is done the credibility of Jung's hypothesis remains.

Jung comments: "These and other experiences like them were sufficient to give me a clue: it is not a question of a specifically racial heredity, but of a universally human characteristic. Nor is it a question of *inherited ideas*, but of a functional disposition to produce the same, or very similar, ideas. This disposition I later called *archetype*." [53]

Jung considered it possible that some of these archetypal patterns could be transmitted by tradition and migration, but that the transmission by heredity was an essential hypothesis because these archetypal images may be produced spontaneously, that is apart from tradition and migration.

Jung's research into the structure of the mind—if the term *structure* be permitted—was mainly in his day to day work in the treatment of patients, and particularly in the analysis of their dreams. In addition to the dreams which clearly referred to the personal experience and life of his patient, he constantly came across dreams with an impersonal quality or content which were inexplicable on a personal level but which became clear when considered in terms of the collective unconscious. Dream-analysis was of paramount importance in Jung's method of treatment and we turn to this subject in the next chapter.

4

DREAMS

Children's dreams, mentioned in the previous chapter, have a special interest because the child is still close to the world whence it came—the primordial world of the unconscious. When Jung was a child he was impressed by a dream he had at the age of four. He never forgot this dream and it remained impressive, a momentous event, although he did not understand it at all when it occurred. Even as a child he felt he must not speak of it.

Until Jung was twelve his father was in charge of the church above the Rhine Fall, near Schaffhausen in northern Switzerland. His home, the pastor's house, was beside the church. He dreamt he was alone in the field close to their house where he usually played, when, to his surprise, he noticed a square hole in the ground. Filled with curiosity, he looked into the hole and saw a flight of stone steps; down these he went slowly, with hesitation. At the bottom was a door covered with a green curtain, which he pulled aside. To his amazement he saw a large, rectangular room with stone walls; a strip of red carpet stretched from the door to the opposite end, where there was a dais with steps, and upon it a big chair. It was not an ordinary chair, but a large golden throne with a red cushion, and on it rested what he took to be a tree trunk about twelve feet high. This had a red, fleshy top, a sort of head, yet not shaped as a head, with an opening like the eye of a demonic god. He had never before seen such a thing and had no idea what it could be, but he felt a strong wave of panic. Then he heard his mother calling to him. Her voice was quite clear, as though she were at the entrance to the steps in the field, yet he realized—in the dream—that she was in the house two hundred yards away. "Just look at him," she said, "he is the man-eater."[54] His mother's words terrified him. This was because he associated "the man-eater" with a Jesuit priest, wearing a cassock, whom he had seen recently near their house. Jesuit, in his mind, meant Jesus, and then he thought of Jesus taking the dead to himself. While he did not understand the dream at all it suddenly occurred to him that, as this room was below the surface of the ground, so too there was something mysterious in life in addition to his ordinary experiences.

Such a dream, with its impersonal quality—for it was unrelated to any previous experience—illustrates how close the child is to the world of the unconscious. Impressive dreams seem to occur at important stages of life, as though at such times we draw upon the experience of humanity of which we are a part.

About a week before he died (June 6th 1961) Jung had such a dream: "I saw a big round stone or block of stone in a high place, a high bare place, and on it is inscribed, 'This shall be a sign unto you of wholeness and oneness'." In the same night there was another dream: "There was a square area of trees and all the fibrous roots came up from the ground and surrounded me and gold threads gleamed between the roots."

With this personal note from Jung's own life we turn to the principles upon which dream-analysis rests.

THE DREAM AND THE DREAMER

Since the unconscious is unknown, inevitably we approach every matter in which we are concerned by using our conscious equipment, that is, by means of the functions described earlier (p. 54). So in trying to understand a dream we first consider it from a conscious standpoint and this involves acceptance of the well-founded hypothesis that the mind operates below as well as above the surface of consciousness. Indeed a strong argument in favour of the reality of the unconscious is the fact that we dream. That the dream is a subjective event will hardly be doubted by anyone who gives it a moment's thought. Surprisingly, some question this. How, they ask, can we explain the element of surprise, of pleasure or of terror in a dream if it is a subjective event arising from the dreamer himself? How can the dreamer, at one and the same time, assume the rôle of author, actor and audience of the play which comes from his own mind? Such a question is explained when the hypothesis of mental activity outside consciousness is accepted. Should this be rejected there is no possibility of investigating the dream which must be disregarded as a meaningless conglomeration of memories and fantasy. At first sight the dream is not a promising topic for thoughtful investigation; it has every appearance of being a lot of nonsense. Many other natural phenomena have given this impression until closer investigation revealed the supposedly worthless as valuable. A familiar example is the discovery that the mine-tip contained uranium.

We start then by accepting the dream as a natural phenomenon. It is not dependent upon conscious intention and is quite outside the scope of will-power. It is true that we cannot prove we have had a dream should this be challenged. Verification is out of the question; but then, we ask, who wants such proof? Certainly not the dreamer; for the dreamer, the dream is an incontestable fact.

It is understandable that dreams are not as a rule taken seriously. To begin with the dream may be unclear, and even if it is clear there is a feeling that its meaning (if any) is beyond our comprehension. Certainly for the scientifically minded a dream is thoroughly frustrating; it seems impossible to decipher the riddle in intellectual terms. Yet the dream took place. It is a product of the unconscious, and as such is bound to be of interest to anyone who accepts the fact that the unconscious plays, or may play, a part in nervous illness.

When we come to investigate a dream it is essential to leave aside prejudice and preconceived ideas and to approach the dream as we would approach an unknown object we want to understand. If we consider dreams at all we must have some theory, for only on such a basis can we expect to discover a meaning behind the medley of words and scenes. At the same time it is important to keep an open mind, otherwise we may make the dream fit our hypothesis. It is impossible to demonstrate that all dreams have a meaning, for some remain mysterious after the most careful examination by doctor and patient. On the other hand, many dreams can be understood and can prove their value to the patient by giving him information previously hidden. It is in consequence of such experiences that Jung writes: "No amount of scepticism and criticism has yet enabled me to regard dreams as negligible occurrences. Often enough they appear senseless, but it is obviously we who lack the sense and ingenuity to read the enigmatic message from the nocturnal realm of the psyche . . . Nobody doubts the importance of conscious experience; why then should we doubt the significance of unconscious happenings?"[55]

To help the dreamer to understand his dream is the aim of a psychotherapist treating a patient with neurosis, an illness which comes apparently inexplicably. Without sense or reason—so it seems—the individual finds his life interrupted by anxiety, by fears, by obsessions that bring to naught his conscious intentions. It is here that the dream can be of practical importance. If its meaning is grasped it can supplement the apparent impotence of conscious effort and so-called will-power to cope with the symptoms.

A dream does not hang in mid-air; it is the property of a particular dreamer, and it is essential that the dreamer should be known as an individual by the therapist whose job it is to co-operate with him so that he may become more aware of himself and the significance of his symptoms. Therefore a careful history of the dreamer's life and his personal and family situation is a first step. As the dream describes the inner situation it must be considered alongside the living person. For the doctor to grasp the meaning, or what he thinks to be the meaning of a dream, is no help to the patient. He must take the patient along with him. By their combined efforts the patient comes to accept responsibility for his unconscious which, after all, is a part of himself.

". . . the dream comes in as the expression of an involuntary unconscious psychic process beyond the control of the conscious mind. It shows the inner truth and reality of the patient as it really is: not as I conjecture it to be, and not as he would like it to be, but *as it is*."[56]

In every-day life we should never think of making a judgment about a person from one or two isolated facts. Similarly it is unwise to jump to conclusions from the analysis of one or two dreams. A single dream of striking intensity can be a highly important event; even so, its meaning will be all the clearer when a number of dreams have been analysed and when the patient and the doctor have had time for further reflection. It often happens that a later dream has a bearing on an earlier one. Dreams should be written down and read over now and then. This appreciation of dreams was constantly advised by Jung who looked on his own dreams with considerable respect.

DREAM-ANALYSIS IN PSYCHOTHERAPY

(a) Initial

It is a matter of observation that a person starting treatment for a nervous illness may find the first visit to the doctor of special importance. Probably it is his first interview with a psychiatrist and he hardly knows what to expect. Almost certainly he will have heard of analysis, and he may have mixed feelings about it. In this new and unclear situation the unconscious, as well as the conscious mind, appears to be activated. Should the analyst ask—and if he doesn't he should!—about dreams, and particularly about recent dreams, he will often find that his patient has had a dream the night before. This happens so regularly that such a dream is known as an *initial dream.* Bearing in mind what has been said about drawing conclusions from isolated dreams, this initial dream should nevertheless be noted, for frequently it seems to bring into focus matters of special importance.

A woman of thirty-five, when asked about dreams at her first interview, said that she had had a dream the previous night. In the dream she was in a tropical country and found herself alone in an enclosure surrounded by a stockade. The enclosure was in a forest but she could say nothing about its purpose. She was impressed by the fact that she was alone. Clearly the stockade was serving some purpose of defence and this seemed very necessary because outside were a variety of wild animals; she noticed particularly a lion and one or two tigers; there was also a hippopotamus close by. As she looked over the stockade she saw that all these animals were watching her and she woke in alarm.

Her problems were associated with her emotional life and she was very shy when meeting men. As the dream was discussed it became obvious to her that the instincts, especially her sexual instinct, and other parts of her personality—represented in the dream by a mixed group of wild animals—were not under control, or at all events not under her conscious control, and so they were felt to be dangerous and had to be excluded.

Later she had another dream which contained echoes of the initial dream: the scene was an English farmyard. Outside were domestic animals—cows, sheep and horses. Noticing that the gate of the farmyard was open she strolled out amongst the animals and found they took no notice of her. Almost casually she happened to observe a bull in the field, but it paid no attention to her. As treatment continued she saw that her attitude towards her instinctive life was based on a series of misunderstandings and her problem had been condensed in the initial dream, in which she protected herself from the wild, but natural sides of her own personality.

"It frequently happens," said Jung, "at the very beginning of treatment that a dream will reveal to the doctor, in broad perspective, the whole programme of the unconscious."[57]

No regular rule can be laid down: the initial dreams may point to the present situation in life, such as work, marriage or current events of any kind. Again, the content of the dream may seem to look ahead or to give a picture of strange events which have no meaning either for the dreamer or the doctor. Sometimes the initial dream has collective (impersonal) features as well as personal material. As a fragment of psychic activity, over which we have no control, the dream is unlikely to meet our conscious expectations.

(b) Recurrent

Recurrent dreams are frequent in youth, but they occur at any age and may persist for years. Broadly speaking the recurrent dream indicates a recurrent problem, especially when the emotional tone is marked and the dreamer wakes up as the situation nears a climax. These dreams are always associated with an unrecognised or unconscious problem or possibility. For instance, a recurrent dream of missing the train, of failing in an examination, of flying, of discovering a room in one's house never seen before, and other typical situations, indicate activity in the unconscious almost crying out to be investigated.

A man in his early forties had a recurrent dream, regularly repeated since the start of his business career in a bank when he was twenty years of age. In the dream he was locking up his house before going to bed when he became aware of a figure outside the window trying to break in. He managed to fasten the window in time, but the would-be intruder moved on to the next window and he dashed along to close it—just in the nick of time. This race continued until they reached a door where the intruder outstripped him and burst in. At this point the dreamer woke with a start. He was rather amused at this dream and it was often recounted as a family joke. That it had any significance never occurred to him. Even without knowing anything about the dreamer it might have been possible to form some opinion about the meaning of the dream, though this would be an unwise proceeding. On enquiry it turned out that he was a most punctilious person; he liked banking because it was so exact. He got great satisfaction in balancing his money each day, as though this was a personal achievement, "something accomplished, something done", and he was, in fact, very capable at his work. Everything in his life seemed to be in order, yet to his surprise his private life was unhappy.

He had become bad tempered and was afraid of being alone, particularly in his own house. He thought of his house very much as he thought of himself: everything about it was carefully planned, everything worked and the garden was well cared for. When the dream was looked at with these associated facts in mind it was seen that the house, with its various divisions such as the kitchen, the living rooms and the more private apartments, represented his personality. In the dream, as he rushed round locking up, he was surprised that the house was much larger than he expected—larger than life in fact, for he lived in a modest suburban dwelling.

Here then, in the dream, we have a picture showing parts of his personality that he simply did not know—because they were unconscious. As the dream is the dreamer, it was necessary also to discover what part of himself was represented by the nefarious figure outside the window: was he really as perfect as he considered himself to be? His wife saw another side of him, and found him extremely trying. So the dream, repeated over years, was nature's endeavour to show another aspect of his personality; but he had brushed it aside as "only a dream"

(c) Anticipatory

This applies particularly to the group of dreams which seem to anticipate the future. "But just as our conscious thoughts often occupy themselves with the future and its possibilities, so do the unconscious and its dreams. There has long been a general belief that the chief function of dreams is prognostication of the future. In antiquity, and as late as the Middle Ages, dreams played their part in medical prognosis."[58]

Jung gives an example from his own experience: "Several months before my mother's death, in September 1922, I had a dream which presaged it."[59] In November 1955 Mrs. Jung was seriously ill and the possibility of recovery was doubtful. Jung had a dream in which he was talking to family friends already dead. No details were mentioned, but the dream, he said, confirmed his worst fears. His wife died a few days later.

As we have seen (p. 75) a dream foreshadowed Jung's concept of the collective unconscious. From such an experience the claim may be made that the dream was prophetic—indeed this has happened when the dreamer has lacked critical judgment. Jung made no such claim. All the same, he often felt that anticipatory dreams might point to future possibilities. He made no dogmatic statement on the matter since, of course, he knew that proof, for or against, was out of the question. Nevertheless, he gave a good deal of attention to dreams of this type. He believed that anticipatory dreams ". . . are no more prophetic than a medical diagnosis or a weather forecast. They are merely an anticipatory combination of probabilities which may coincide with the actual behaviour of things but need not necessarily agree in every detail."[60]

Whether the dream was of an initial, recurrent, or anticipatory type, Jung assumed that, as it occurred in the present, it was important for the present. Consequently we must have a complete picture of the dreamer's current situation. Of the unconscious we know nothing from moment to moment beyond the fact that it is a part of the total psyche composed of conscious and unconscious. Experience in dream-analysis—our main source of information about the unconscious—suggests that the dream may provide information to supplement the conscious attitude. In consequence of this new point of view the dreamer may reconsider his current motives and actions. Jung often got a hint from a dream when he knew the patient well, and would call his attention to certain possibilities. Often such hints were very much to the point.

SELF-REGULATION IN DREAMS

Jung's nearest approach to a theory of dreams is that the psyche is a self-regulating system, that is, a compensatory mechanism operates between the conscious and the unconscious. This is a principle in dream interpretation which has stood the test of time and has been accepted widely by psychotherapists. In studying a patient's dream the therapist should always consider what conscious attitude may be compensated by the dream. Jung, of course, made it clear that compensation could not be observed as an automatic process in every single dream. It was necessary to study a series of dreams and in looking over them the process of compensation might be observed. As was pointed out earlier (p. 84) the circumstances of the dreamer's everyday life must be kept in mind all the time, for compensation, an automatic process, is taking place in the natural course of events, and the dream must be seen in relation to the conscious attitude.

Compensation, like any other adaptation in the mind and body, may be upset, and when that occurs unhappiness in the form of anxieties and other distress of mind appears. Jung gives credit to Alfred Adler for introducing the concept of compensation into the psychology of the neurosis. Adler considered that an individual having a feeling of inferiority compensated for this by developing a fictional goal of superiority analogous to the compensation effected in the body when there is a deformity or bodily inadequacy. Jung went much further and taught that a general functional adjustment was going on, or tending to go on, all the time. He was considerably influenced by parts of the teaching of Heraclitus, the Greek philosopher who flourished about 500 B.C. Heraclitus produced an imaginative hypothesis. This was his doctrine of eternal flux, uninterrupted motion and change. All comes and goes, from life death, from death life. When a one-sided attitude persists, inevitably the opposite attitude comes to the fore in an automatic attempt to restore a balanced attitude. This to and fro process, which governs what may seem to be chance occurrence, Heraclitus called the rule of *enantiodromia*, a tendency towards the opposite (*enantios*, opposite, and *dromos*, a quick movement). Nothing remains fixed, permanent, unaltered. Everywhere in life we see "the ever-whirling wheel of Change". Life is a contest of opposites: birth and death; health and sickness; love and hate; giving and taking; systole and diastole; summer and winter; day and night. In the ancient doctrine of Nemesis, the personification of divine justice that could not permit any wrong to go unpunished, we find the same "law" expressed. Proverbs of all nations also strike this note: more haste, less speed; pride goes before a fall, and so on indefinitely.

It should be noted that the term *opposites* does not mean opposition in the sense that there is a fight between two parts of the mind in which one might be victorious. Both sides are necessary in the operation of the mind as elsewhere in life. Thus we read in *The Times* 27.11.65, "Political vitality does eventually depend on having a vigorous opposition." Negative and positive when used together are valuable, apart they are valueless. In every part of Jung's psychology the concept of mental energy appears as a play of compensating opposites.

A literary example, described by Jung as a classical type of compensation, is found in H. G. Wells' *Christina Alberta's Father*: "Mr. Preemby, a midget personality, discovers that he is really a reincarnation of Sargon, King of Kings."[61] Jung remarks that this example of compensation is "taken from life so to speak". This enigmatic comment refers to the fact that on a visit to London Jung had dinner with H. G. Wells at his house in Regent's Park. After dinner the conversation turned to the peculiarities of mental illness. Wells asked Jung what really happened in the mind of a person who developed schizophrenia and became delusional. Jung described the course of a schizophrenic illness with delusional features and explained that these arose through projection. (In projection ideas originating in one's own mind are attributed to other people, or to events apart from oneself.) Wells was deeply interested and Jung was amazed to notice that in his intense concentration he seemed visibly to "shrink back in his chair as though sucking in my words in a most incredible way". Previously Wells had been expansive and they had had a wonderfully good dinner. After Jung had finished talking—and he said he talked for about half the evening—Wells became expansive again. This talk, with considerable elaboration, became the theme of *Christina Alberta's Father*.

In the treatment of neurosis by dream-analysis the concept of compensation is most useful. It can be explained to the patient in simple terms and examples abound in everyday life. At the same time, it is difficult to know exactly what takes place in the process of compensation, nor is it necessary that we should. Jung "went by experience", as he put it, in formulating his views on compensation, as every serious worker must until the operation of the body-mind unit is understood.

COMPENSATION: MENTAL AND PHYSICAL

Compensation within the mind may be compared to a compensator, that is a mechanical device which keeps a machine at a certain rate of motion in order to achieve and retain its optimum efficiency. As might be expected the same principle of compensation is observed to take place in the body through the operation of homeostatic mechanisms which impose a degree of self-regulation within the body. These mechanisms act as compensators to preserve uniformity and stability at a favourable level. Should this mechanism become impaired, health is threatened and illness appears. Sometimes the symptoms of illness can be seen as an effort to set matters right. Unfortunately this is not always successful and may require to be supplemented by medical treatment. Such treatment is (or should be) based on a knowledge of the physiology and biochemistry of the body and its aim is to restore compensation or balance. In the mind as in the body self-regulation, by compensation, works automatically until it is upset by our response to unusual circumstances, or by changes in the body. Many attempts have been made, and will continue to be made, to correct mental unrest and improve the state of mind by the use of drugs. These have been shown to be valuable in relieving depression for instance; but their application is far from exact and it is not certain how they operate or at what point in the bodily activity they are designed to act.

Knowledge, or even tentative knowledge, of how the mind works is essential as a basis in psychotherapy. Such knowledge is similar to that required in treating sickness of the body; but there is an important difference. While the full co-operation of the patient is useful when employing physical methods, it is not an essential, but in every form of psychotherapy it is vital.

In order to avoid ambiguity it is often necessary to separate certain opposites temporarily—for example, the conscious attitude and the unconscious as revealed, possibly in a dream—in order to make matters comprehensible to a patient. But that there are such opposites should be discussed later with the patient, otherwise the separation may be carried too far and the complementary opposite may be overlooked. This can lead to an unfortunate one-sidedness. Dreams, as the main source of information from the unconscious, must be used if we are to know anything about the inner, unconscious life of the dreamer. An analyst must be familiar with the dreamer's life and circumstances, and with his impressions of himself. Thus questions are asked such as: What sort of a person are you when you are quite well? How has the breakdown changed you? The answers give direct information about the ego-consciousness. That, however, is not enough. If compensation is brought about by the reciprocal interaction of the conscious and unconscious, it is essential to gather as much information as possible from dreams. Treatment on the conscious level by good advice and encouragement is no doubt helpful up to a point. Most patients have had more than enough "treatment" of this type before undertaking the more prolonged treatment by analysis which always relies, in its efforts to cure, upon the co-operation of the unconscious. This was Jung's experience, and it was on this basis that he practised dream-analysis and found that the conscious understanding and acceptance of the dreams provided the necessary compensation and facilitated the self-regulation of the psyche. To those who know little of psychotherapy and psychological analysis this may sound easy and perhaps rather interesting. In practice it is different. Hard mutual work by the doctor and his patient is required. It can be interesting, but it is not amusing and it demands sincerity and intelligence.

COMPENSATION IN ANALYSIS

In considering the subject of dreams it might reasonably be remarked by the so-called practical man-in-the-street that he had not time to speculate about dreams. Such a remark is not so full of common-sense as it may seem. Jung's research into the structure of the mind arose from the necessity of helping his patients who "for no reason at all" developed a nervous breakdown. Patients with such a complaint are, to their distress, aware of its irrational qualities. Dreams may appear senseless; but experience shows that dream-analysis is indispensable in the treatment of neurosis.

Jung's typology contains a description of the general attitude types of extraversion and introversion, and an account of the functions of thinking, feeling, sensation and intuition (p. 54). When this is taken in conjunction with his teaching on the unconscious it provides a method of treatment which those who have used it know to be valuable. Here the concept of compensation should be borne in mind. As neurosis is the result of an over-emphasis or under-emphasis of certain features in the personality, we have in Jung's typology a method of making a fairly accurate assessment of the conscious attributes. We infer that what is absent, or under-developed, in consciousness will be found in the unconscious. In such a situation an awareness of the pairs of opposites, conscious and unconscious, extravert-introvert, will help us to consider the dreams in an intelligent manner. It helps, also, to remind us that the psyche works as a whole, and that while time is devoted to the analysis of dreams, the analyst and his patient should remember that everything in the mind is present all the time, even though the greater part will necessarily be out of sight at any particular moment. We are only conscious of that which is in the focus of consciousness. In point of fact although the field of consciousness may seem limited, the process of perception, that is knowledge gained by the use of the senses, is more than a recording of sensations. It is an active proceeding, governed by memory of similar percep-tions, and so, apparently automatically (that is by way of the unconscious), an interpretation of the sensory perception takes place.

Nothing is gained by the mere knowledge that a person is an extravert or an introvert. It is the exaggeration of one or other which leads to trouble, and it is through the study of dreams that the one-sidedness becomes evident and so, under our conscious direction, capable of adjust-ment and regulation. Provided the dreamer's inner situa-tion is made conscious through psychological treatment, he can add his own efforts to those of nature which through the symptoms of the neurosis is making an attempt to redress the balance.

Self-regulation and compensation must always be thought of in relation to the person's everyday life. And it is important, also, to avoid preconceived ideas of the lines along which adjustment is to take place. There is a tendency to think of compensation as working at maximum efficiency towards fulfilment of life. But life does not go on indefinitely, and at times the compensation seems to indicate a preparation for death. Dreams at times can strike a gloomy note. An illustration is that of an elderly woman who had a dream in which a tiger was attacking a black horse. The horse was lying on its back and the tiger was tearing out its intestines. When asked about the dream she said she was alarmed at it although she could not make any sense of it. As the dreamer was in hospital preparing for an operation for a malignant disease of the stomach, it was impossible to think of the dream as striking a favourable note or making a compensation which would lead to her adjustment. Here again, however, it would be unwise to take a single dream as representing the whole situation.

"BIG" DREAMS

Dreams vary in their importance to the dreamer, as in waking life not every thought is momentous. Yet the seeming simplicity of certain dreams may be deceptive. To explain a dream as caused by an event the day before is perhaps tempting; but we can be mistaken. Although items in the dream may resemble the activity of the previous day, there may be marked differences. The incidents of yesterday may be used in the symbolism of the dream, yet the dream is not therefore merely a muddled recollection of events that have just occurred.

Sometimes, but not always, the opinion of the dreamer may decide whether the dream is or is not significant. In some cases the impact of the dream is so clear that it cannot be overlooked. Amongst such dreams are those that are recounted to others during the day as though they were of more than personal importance. When Jung spent some months with the Elgoni, a people living in the jungles of Elgon in East Africa, he learnt that they paid close attention to dreams. If the dream appeared to be of a personal nature it was disregarded; if it was what they called a "big" dream, then the other members of the tribe were called together to hear it, for it had a general (i.e. collective) rather than a personal meaning. Jung was much impressed by hearing this remarkable and unexpected confirmation of his theory that there is both a personal and a collective unconscious. He comments on the "big" or "meaningful" dreams: they do not come from the personal, but from a deeper level, that is from the collective unconscious. "They reveal their significance —quite apart from the subjective impression they make— by their plastic form, which often has a poetic force and beauty. Such dreams occur mostly during the critical phases of life, in early youth, puberty, at the onset of middle age (thirty-six to forty), and within sight of death."[62]

AMPLIFICATION

Jung's word association experiments (p. 25) showed the importance of the complex as an indicator of unconscious mental activity. An indicator, however, is not the dream and the dream is the goal. Since the complex is the hidden emotional content of the dream, it determines the structure of the dream and so cannot be separated from it; but complexes often become personified in our dreams and naturally they are not recognised. They appear as unknown people with easily described characteristics, so-called splinter or broken-off bits of the psyche, operating, as it were, on their own. In addition to these personal features we find, though not in every dream, archetypal material relevant to the compensatory aim of the dream.

We ask for the dreamer's impressions of the dream: what strikes him as significant; what is the atmosphere of the dream—was it agreeable, alarming, interesting or featureless? In this way through his associations about the items in the dream we see in what context the dream lies.

This simple method of finding out about each part of the dream is known as *amplification*. By its use the dreamer is able to see the dream in the setting of other events in his life, and at the same time the analyst learns something more of the dreamer. This is how we would approach any unknown phenomenon. At the same time we should ask ourselves the question, mentioned earlier: What conscious attitude does the dream compensate? As the doctor is presumed—by the patient—to know what the dream means, he should explain that he does not know and that his only way of finding out is through the participation of the patient in the treatment.

It should be noted that amplification is carried out on a conscious level. This is in contrast to the therapeutic procedure of free-association, devised by Freud, in which the patient, relaxing on a couch, speaks of the first thing that comes into his mind and so allows the unconscious to express itself. Jung's criticism of this passive method was that inevitably it leads to the patient's complexes and the dream may not be mentioned. Free-association, as the term implies, may lead anywhere and a dream is not required to set it going. As the dream has a bearing on the situation at that time and is the concurrent contribution of the unconscious, it is likely to be important and should be noted. Hence the active intervention to make sure that the message of the unconscious is not side-tracked. Dream-analysis is always co-operative as the intervention of the analyst shows. Naturally it is valuable to know of the complex or complexes; but it is also important to understand the dream and to discover, if we can, what the unconscious has to say about the complex. That is why dream-analysis, using the procedure of amplification, is given a central place in Analytical Psychology.

Amplification by means of the dreamer's associations is adequate so long as the content of the dream is on a personal level. Not infrequently, however, the dreamer is unable to give any associations. This happens when the dream is of an impersonal, collective character. Then the associations and observations of the analyst are relevant. By his knowledge of anthropology, of mythology, fairy tales and folk-lore, the analyst may be able to throw light on the dream. Such knowledge is part of the equipment an analyst acquires by his professional training for analytical work. Experience shows that such specialised knowledge often "clicks" with the patient and that is how we know whether or not the dream has significance for the dreamer.

Another feature to be noted about dream-analysis is that the dream is not looked upon merely as an instrument to be used in the process of analysis. Dream life is part of the living experience of the individual and as such it is to be valued. With the co-operation of the patient the process of dream-interpretation can reach beyond the bounds of active treatment for the relief of symptoms. Dreams can and should be used by the patient himself when the analytical treatment has finished.

5

OUR INNER WORLD

DREAMS AND RESEARCH

From the investigation of dreams we may get the impression of the unconscious as an almost limitless field of exploration with boundaries beyond the capacity of an individual. This is a better attitude of mind than complacency. After all, our knowledge of consciousness— our own ego-consciousness—is far from complete. Nevertheless a beginning has been made in the application of psychological ideas in the treatment of mental ill-health. Jung was always modest in his claims, and he points out that "psychology is one of the youngest sciences".[63] At the same time we have good reason to expect development. Originally a branch of philosophy, psychology, relying chiefly on the empirical method, has grown rapidly over the last hundred years. Significant advances have followed the various attempts to understand unconscious mental activity. Where these have been successful, psychiatrists and others concerned with mental health and mental sickness have been able to do their work in a more intelligent manner. Jung, as a young doctor, found hypnotism a failure in getting any notion of unconscious mental activity. His rewarding work in experimental research was mentioned earlier (p. 25). To his surprise this soon provided plenty of evidence of unconscious activity in the formation of the complex. Jung considers that Freud's "unique merit lies in his discovery of a method for exploring the unconscious and, more particularly, dreams . . . I do not wish to belittle Freud's achievement but I feel I must be fair to all those who . . . have laid the foundations without which neither Freud nor myself would have been able to accomplish our tasks. Thus Pierre Janet, August Forel, Théodore Flournay, Morton Prince, Eugen Bleuler, deserve gratitude and remembrance whenever we speak of the first steps of medical psychology."[64]

Jung's later research, after his experimental work with the word-association tests, was mainly upon the subject of the collective unconscious and the ways in which this hypothesis throws light on the problems of contemporary life and, notably, upon the treatment of patients with illness of the mind. Writing of the collective unconscious, Jung claims that ". . . every human child is possessed of a ready-made system of adapted psychic functioning prior to all consciousness."[65]

Taking the psyche as a natural phenomenon, and dreams as a manifestation of unconscious creative activity, Jung began systematic observation of the contents of dreams, and particularly their collective features. This was a difficult bit of work, for his rôle was that of an explorer. It may sound like a mystical venture into an abstract world of the imagination. In fact it was a serious effort to understand the strange material produced by his patients, and by others who were healthy, for dreams are the experience of all.

To get Jung, as a person, into focus, the reader may be interested to know what sort of a man he was. Those who knew him and had opportunities of seeing him in his private life, as opposed to the lecture room, found him a very practical person with a ready sense of humour and with the gift of making his guest aware that he was accepted on equal terms. In his early years he was fond of mountaineering, and keen on sailing on the Lake of Zürich, a large lake surrounded by hills, so that sailing called for alertness and resource. When his family were young, weekends were spent camping on the shores of the upper part of the Zürich Lake, not far from the place where subsequently he built what was to be a week-end house, near Bollingen. He took part in the actual building of this house, known as the Tower. Life there was simple, almost primitive. That is how Jung wanted it. He liked being near the earth and doing everything that needed to be done, such as cutting the wood, cooking the meals, and even digging the potatoes. He had his feet on the ground in more ways than one.

When he took up the systematic study of the un-conscious his patients' needs were his main consideration: he was determined to find out what their symptoms meant, where they originated and how they could be cured. Early in his career he realised that the study of conscious activity was most important—hence his typology, described in

Chapter 2. But it was only worth while if associated with research into the unconscious. He could never think of the mind as partitioned; it was a conscious/unconscious unit.

His investigations into the psychology of the dream naturally led on to fuller study of such contents of the unconscious as became available. As a physician he had an obligation to find out what he could about the inner world of the mind. He was keen to understand the symptoms his patients complained of, so he listened most carefully to what they had to say. It was the same in ordinary conversation—he made sure that he knew what people were talking about. This had nothing to do with the language used, for he was an expert linguist. When his patients recounted their dreams they were often surprised at first that he took them seriously, for usually they thought their dreams were rather silly and not worth mentioning. Jung asked his patients to write out their dreams and to think about them. No encouragement was given to those who produced a dream and asked him what it meant, not having given it a thought themselves.

ACTIVE IMAGINATION

Through the analysis of dreams an effort was made to understand in what way the ego, the focussing point in consciousness, was related to the contents of the unconscious. Fantasy and imagination are not always differentiated in Jung's writings and this can be confusing. Imagination is usually described as the process of forming a picture in the mind of something not perceived by the senses—an experience everyone has had. Jung sometimes used the word "fantasy" in this sense; but as a rule the intended meaning was obvious from the context. He was careful to draw a sharp distinction between fantasy and *active imagination*.

"A fantasy is more or less your own invention, and remains on the surface of personal things and conscious expectations. But active imagination, as the term denotes, means that the images have a life of their own and that the symbolic events develop according to their own logic—that is, of course, if your conscious reason does not interfere."[66]

Very often the conscious mind does interfere with the creative imagination, as Coleridge knew to his cost when he was interrupted as he was eagerly writing down a vivid dream. There remained only the fragment, known as *Kubla Khan*. Everyone has the experience of being in a "brown study" or day-dream, a period of abstracted musing which comes unsought and is put aside as valueless when we "come to", and our conscious mind takes over. Something is active in the mind at such a time, and it must be the unconscious for it is not the same as conscious thinking as everyone knows. Jung thought that if we could train ourselves to induce this frame of mind it should be possible to contact the unconscious in a conscious state. With practice it is possible to concentrate upon a mental picture and the image in our mind begins to alter and to move, or even to take the place of the stream of consciousness. Naturally there is a tendency to think that we are deluding ourselves and that there is nothing there—we are making it up; it is not really the unconscious. Yet it has numerous resemblances to the experience of dreaming, which is certainly not our own invention. In conscious life we rely upon the unconscious, to a greater extent than we realise, to provide us with material for even an ordinary conversation. That is why we often surprise ourselves by what we say and we may even be impressed by the admirable (or regrettable) ideas that appear in our minds "from nowhere"—our way of describing the unconscious.

A "brown study" or a day-dream seems at first glance a flimsy basis for serious research. We should remember, however, that ideas "come into our head" and may throw a new light on some of our practical every-day problems. We cannot count on the arrival of these helpful ideas; they are unpredictable. Nevertheless when they come we have been in touch with our unconscious, even though it is only for a few seconds. But, thought Jung, why need the period of contact be so brief? Perhaps it could be extended if we were in the right frame of mind—relaxed, uncritical and prepared to see what happens. This turned out to be the case and from this simple beginning developed what came to be known as active imagination or the technique of active imagination. This did not displace but supplemented amplification.

Writing of active imagination, Jung says: "It is true that there are unprofitable, futile, morbid and unsatisfying fantasies whose sterile nature is immediately recognised by every person endowed with common sense; but the faulty performance proves nothing against the normal performance. All the works of man have their origin in creative imagination. . . . Coming back to the question of my technique, I ask myself how far I am indebted to Freud for its existence. At all events I learned it from Freud's method of free association, and I regard it as a direct extension of that."[67]

Jung did not consider it suitable for every patient and

it was used only in the later stages of analysis, and with those who were stable. One great advantage was that such patients could use it alone when reflecting on their dreams or other matters.

When we are able to concentrate upon the inner current of ideas then our unconscious can produce remarkable images and thoughts. Sometimes the pictures arising from active imagination replace dreams, although this is not very frequent. Active imagination may be used in dream-analysis, particularly if the analysis of the dream has opened up some new topic which may need a sustained effort to learn its meaning. There is no fixed rule about using active imagination and the analyst will be guided by the patient's stability, capacity for co-operation and common sense. Often the unconscious imagery is fleeting and then it is helpful to let active imagination express itself by spontaneous painting, drawing and modelling. This excellent means of tapping the hidden world of the unconscious is not appreciated sufficiently. No definite goal is in sight; the imagination takes over and guides the hand, apart altogether from conscious intention.

Only the uninitiated ask what the picture means. They seem to think that the picture is worthless unless it can be understood intellectually. It is not necessary for the artist to believe in his picture; it would never occur to him to think in such terms. He relies on feeling. For him it may have no clear meaning or intention; yet he enjoyed painting it; he values it—not for its artistic worth but for the sense of freedom or of achievement accompanying its production. Painting the picture or modelling in clay is like a voyage of discovery into the inner world of the psyche. On the way, moods, previously puzzling, can be apprehended because their meaning has been felt, seen in a flash—a flash of intuitive understanding. The effect of this creative activity is not diminished by the fact that the artist has no idea what the picture or model means intellectually; he is not thinking logically. Meaning may be the language of science; but life is not always under the guidance of pure reason.

Active imagination, when used successfully, helps us to become aware of the unconscious in consciousness; whereas in a dream the unconscious material is usually obscure, and may require considerable analysis, by amplification and in other ways, before we can discover its significance. But, to repeat, active imagination is neither better nor worse than dream-analysis. Each method is good and each must be used with discrimination as the occasion requires. As the product of active imagination is before us in a conscious state, possibly expressed in a painting, it is generally more easily assimilated as it is more coherent. This may seem complicated; but in practice it is simple enough, and rarely presents any difficulty once the principles have been grasped.

SPONTANEOUS ART

Painting or modelling is a valuable adjunct to psychotherapy. To apply paint and to find a picture developing has the quality of a creative act which comes as a series of surprises to the artist. Those who have never tried spontaneous painting cannot judge its effects. It is by no means a new idea and it was widely used long before Jung was born. And such work really is spontaneous: there is no going by rules, beyond learning how to mix the paint. Once this stage is over, natural endowment takes over, for training is not necessary. Concentration on what is being drawn seems to release one's energy; it becomes vitalised, as though directed from the unconscious. Conscious direction plays a minor part. Jung found that spontaneous art was of genuine assistance to patients in expressing the mood of a dream, or in active imagination. Through the painting (or modelling) the "feeling" of the unconscious becomes a reality. This unlooked for experience is often mentioned by those who previously had thought of the unconscious as an abstract psychological term. To feel it had reality for them puts matters on a different level. It is in such experiences that spontaneous art proves its practical worth. We cannot look directly at the unconscious as at an object. Yet it can be experienced through active imagination in the spontaneous act of painting, modelling, drawing or wood carving. Any medium is suitable.

Jung himself used painting in working over his own dreams, and so knew its value. He writes: "We have only to look at the drawings and paintings of patients who supplement their analysis by active imagination to see that colours are feeling-values. Mostly, to begin with, only a pencil or pen is used to make rapid sketches of dreams, sudden ideas, and fantasies. But from a certain moment . . . the patients begin to make use of colour . . . merely intellectual interest gives way to emotional participation. Occasionally the same phenomenon can be observed in dreams, which at such moments are dreamt in colour, or a particularly vivid colour is insisted upon."[68] After some practice it is comparatively easy to let the picture develop "on its own". Children paint imaginative pictures without prompting; adults are usually more sophisticated and at first find it difficult to be quite natural.

He continues: "Giving form to what is unformed has a specific effect in cases where the conscious attitude offers an overcrowded unconscious no possible means of expressing itself."[69]

It is in such circumstances that the element of surprise in painting is so arresting. Perhaps the painting is begun with no end in view and then it begins to take shape, form, and thereby comes alive, and does express something that cannot be expressed in words. It is the language of feeling and emotion. No one should doubt the importance of being in touch with our emotional life which so often determines success and failure in our ventures.

A SEMINAR BY JUNG

In January 1952 Jung gave a seminar to a number of psychiatrists and others, in the dining room of his house in Küsnacht, upon a series of eleven pictures which had been used a few days earlier to illustrate a lecture at the C. G. Jung Institute in Zürich. Jung had not been at the lecture, but he had discussed the case-material and had been particularly interested in it, especially in the paintings done by a girl of twenty. She had the unusual experience of seeing her double, that is an autoscopic (seeing one's self) phenomenon, often described in fiction, but seldom mentioned in psychiatric literature as patients with such symptoms are rare. In describing the phenomenon of the double (double-ganger, Doppelgänger) some writers use the expression "mirror image". Certainly there was no "mirror image" in this example. Though the autoscopic representation resembled the original closely, the girl herself said that she often "saw herself outside herself" and it usually frightened her because of the differences between the vision and her own body. There were many such experiences. One took place during a walk with a friend: "I felt completely outside myself; that I had dissolved and become a part of all that was around—lake, trees, lights, the sky, in fact the whole atmosphere. I was looking at something that wasn't really happening. Then I saw E (her friend) walking with a girl who seemed just a body, her face expressionless, her eyes fixed on the horizon; I felt that only her outward appearance existed and that her arms, her legs and her whole body were hollow. They walked toward me in a kind of stupor, and as they came near me I felt a shudder go through my whole body and I became the girl who was walking with E. I was afraid that this other being was watching and I kept looking behind and all around hoping, yet fearing, that I might find it. I was breathing very deeply and walking clumsily. I felt sick."

Dissimilarity between the vision and the actual body of the girl ruled out the "mirror-image" idea.

Here we have a projection of a partial aspect of the personality in the form of a visible image, representing a distinctive attitude of mind in the individual whose double it is. In another example the patient seemed to leave her body and pictured herself standing inside the window of her room with her back to the glass. She described herself as expressionless with empty eye-sockets.

In the course of the girl's treatment in hospital she painted a number of pictures; they seemed to form a bridge with the unconscious and the therapeutic effect was beneficial; they threw light on obscure features in her illness.

In commenting on the pictures Jung began by asking, "What would you expect the unconscious to be doing in such an illness?" And the answer was: producing a compensation. He then picked out features in certain of the pictures which conformed closely with the girl's psychology and this was possible as some of the pictures contained symbolism of a collective nature.

Without the pictures as a bridge, psychological treatment would have been almost impossible. When Jung was examining the pictures he asked what the prognosis (outlook) was for the girl's recovery. Told that it was not bright, he pointed to one picture showing the girl holding an open cage in her right hand as though to invite a bird, flying above, to return to the cage, and said, "She is doing just what the medicine men do in Africa—open the cage at night so that the souls which escape in the night may be caught and restored to their owners. This is a beautiful picture and shows that something might be done." (Opening the cage: this refers to the belief held by some primitive people that during sleep the soul escapes from the body. By using a cage it was thought that the medicine man could re-capture the errant soul and return it to its owner.)

Jung's "hunch" that something might be done for the girl turned out to be true. After a long illness she recovered. An account of this girl's illness with some of Jung's comments appeared in a volume, *Festschrift*, published on the occasion of Jung's eightieth birthday.[70]

FIGURES IN THE UNCONSCIOUS

THE PERSONA

A constant interchange occurs between the conscious and the unconscious and there is no fixed division between them. We cannot anticipate our thoughts; quite apart from our conscious wishes unexpected thoughts appear. Also, that which is conscious today may be forgotten or repressed tomorrow. This pattern of thought is the experience of everyone. Nevertheless we retain our identity, our awareness of ourselves; our belief that we know our own mind; our assumption that in spite of everything we are the person we think we are. This, however, is not necessarily true for other people. They may not have the sense of continuity concerning us that we possess. Different characteristics appear at different times: to the onlooker at his place of work a man may be cheerful, forthcoming, and warm-hearted. But in another environment, such as his home, he may be exactly the reverse. "Which, then, is the true character, the real personality?" writes Jung. ". . . even in the normal individual character-splitting is by no means an impossibility."[71]

To begin with the healthy infant is completely natural, without affectation. He accepts and rejects regardless of the feelings of others. As he develops he becomes conscious of other people, and learns by imitation how to conduct himself in a community. Children vary considerably, and so the degree of imitation, and its onset, will be different in every child.

Jung distinguished imitation from identification which is *unconscious imitation*. Should a son identify himself too closely with his father he may lose some of his originality. There are degrees of identification and its strength depends, as far as we know, upon the emotional bond between the child and its parent or parents, or perhaps with a nurse who was devoted to it as a baby. Valuable in many respects, imitation becomes a hindrance when it retards individual development; it may also induce, in the child, a lack of assurance in his own capacities. Identification, being unconscious imitation, operates, of course, without the child's knowledge. It serves a purpose; and yet it, too, becomes a handicap when it tends to build up in the youngster a secondary personality at variance with his true nature. This secondary personality is not without its merits. Different attitudes are required at various times—for instance, at home and in business life. These are necessary adjustments if we are to live in a community. We expect the policeman to behave as a policeman whatever his attitude may be in his family circle. Presumably the policeman has no difficulty in putting aside his official manner when he is off duty. But supposing he cannot dispense with it, then he has become identified with his official rôle, and this is regrettable because it means that he has become separated from part of himself.

Jung employed the term *persona* (mask) to describe the demeanour which corresponded with the requirements of the individual's everyday life. Ordinarily a good deal of flexibility will be needed: the persona of the policeman arresting a thief, helping the injured, giving evidence in court, or dealing with a lost child, are all consistent with his job. If he is a healthy man he will not become identified to a marked degree with any of the parts he is called upon to play in his daily life. This outer attitude, the persona, represents the conscious ego with its numerous variations, and it must not be mistaken for the whole man. Should the individual become identified with his persona, this amounts to a denial of the other parts of the personality, including the unconscious.

When unhealthy identification occurs we may anticipate the appearance of an opposite in the dreams. An example of this occurs in the dream mentioned on p. 88. That the intruder was the dreamer is beyond question, and his presence represents the aim of the dream to establish compensation, to restore healthy conditions in the mind. In analysis of the dream this would become evident.

THE SHADOW

In dream-analysis an unknown figure of the same sex as the dreamer often appears. An example is the burglar in the dream referred to in the last paragraph. In that dream the unrecognised figure from the dreamer's point of view was evil, undesirable. He was not conscious of this part of his personality and would have disowned it. All the same, it was active. Other people did know it; they encountered it, and reacted by blaming him for his unpleasant ways. He felt misunderstood and lost his temper in trying to justify himself. In the dream we have a dramatization of this situation in which an unfamiliar facet of his nature is brought to his notice, although he failed to see that the dream had anything to do with himself.

This sort of thing happens when the individual has become identified with his persona and neglects the other parts of his personality which then act negatively. This negative side is not always nefarious. There are burglars in real life, and they may look on others and their possessions with criminal intent. In such circumstances their dreams may show a thoroughly decent person as the shadow figure. It would be a mistake to assume that the unconscious is always an unpleasant side of the personality, although it very often is so; and if there is that side, and it is unknown, the health of the mind will be impaired.

It is not usually difficult to bring about adjustment for the concept of the persona and the shadow is easily understood. As the hidden aspect of the ego-consciousness the shadow is a hindrance; but when it is consciously accepted life can alter in unexpected ways.

In defining the attitude types of extraversion and introversion and the functions of thinking, feeling, sensation and intuition, Jung was not giving an exact specification of the operation of the conscious mind, but a general outline which conforms fairly closely to what we find in everyday life. Likewise, the description of the figures in the unconscious, such as the persona and shadow, is not intended to be a guide-book to the mysterious world of the unconscious. These images cannot be defined exactly, nor do they appear in any predictable order. Jung sometimes used the concept of the shadow to include everything in the psyche outside consciousness, that is, the collective as well as the personal unconscious. Thus the shadow, the inner attitude, may also be identical with the soul or *anima* (considered in the next section). This wider aspect of the shadow is mentioned here for the sake of completeness, as the *shadow* is sometimes, mistakenly, spoken of as though it applied only to a part of the personality one prefers to ignore, thus suggesting that it belongs exclusively to the personal unconscious. There is a partial truth in this, for from an analysis of the personal unconscious the shadow can in large measure be inferred. "No one," says Jung, "can become conscious of the shadow without considerable moral effort. To become conscious of it involves recognising the dark aspects of the personality as present and real . . . these have an emotional nature . . . Emotion, incidentally, is not an activity of the individual but something that happens to him . . ." A main difficulty in recognising the shadow is that it is bound up with projections which, being unconscious, are not perceived, and this leads to blaming the other person. "Projections," says Jung, "change the world into the replica of one's own unknown face."[72]

Appreciation by the patient of the need for co-operation in dream-analysis, in the technique of active imagination when it is used, and a capacity to use spontaneous art as part of the amplification procedure, are all of value in making shadow-projections visible—a first step in understanding, in acceptance, and so in adjustment.

THE ANIMA

There are many similarities in the psychology of men and women and everything that has been said about the ego, the persona, and to some extent the shadow, applies to each sex. In textbooks on psychology it seems to be assumed, wrongly, that the psychology of men and women is to all intents and purposes the same. When we come to examine the unconscious of men and of women, by dream-analysis, active imagination or other methods, the differences between masculine and feminine psychology begin to stand out. One of Jung's most valuable contributions to normal psychology, and thence to abnormal psychology, lies in his recognition of the distinctive features in the unconscious of men and of women. In the unconscious of every man there is a feminine element, personified in dreams by a female figure or image, and to this Jung gave the name *anima*, the latin word for "soul" or "breath of life", that which animates. Its counterpart in woman, the *animus*, is personified by a man, or sometimes by men.

It will be convenient to consider first the concept of the anima. In its appearance in dreams it is not, of course, an actual woman, nor even a single image with constant characteristics. Images of the anima vary and, being unconscious, it is likely to be projected on one, or at times on several women, perhaps in succession or even simultaneously. With growing masculinity the boy, and then the youth, may try to put aside what he looks on as feminine qualities. As an infant and in childhood his mother was his natural companion, and therefore his projection of the feminine element in himself fell on her. Ordinarily the mother becomes less and less important to him, although her influence continues as the prototype of all women; she is the first woman he knew and she remains important whether he is conscious of it or not. This, in part, is the origin of his anima qualities. We speak here of the regular course of development. But it may happen that the youth is unable to free himself from his mother because he has developed a mother-complex, that is, his mother has become of intense importance to him. This is liable to happen when his mother is demonstrative, over-affectionate, and his father somewhat remote. Moreover his mother may consider his father as of secondary importance, merely an object to be looked after, perhaps a little more important than the furniture. She clings to the son—often the youngest in the family—while urging him, in due course, to get married and become independent. This he cannot do because his heterosexuality is by now associated with his ideas of his mother.

With the mother-complex there are two sides: the woman who is the perfect mother also sucks the life out of her children because she has no life of her own, whilst every sort of good and noble reason is put forward by the son to prove that he must never leave his mother.

Jung attributes the influences affecting the child (or children) as only in part due to the mother herself. In addition there are the projections of the child upon her, and these have more than a personal significance in so far as they attribute to her an authority greater than she as a person possesses.[73]

In addition to the influence of his mother as a source of the anima there is the inherited image, that is the racial ideas of woman, derived as part of his personality from man's experience of woman in the past. The inherited image of woman always forms part of the anima image in the man's unconscious. He comes into the world adapted for woman, and his direct experience of his mother, building on this inherited quality, enlarges it. Then the boy has the experience of meeting girls and hearing his parents and friends talking about them; he observes the rôle given to girls in his social environment, which varies in different localities or from country to country.

That a man has this image of woman in his mind is a matter of everyday observation and its absence would be abnormal. Infants, whether boys or girls, are brought up in much the same way. After two or three years the boy must become a little man, have his hair cut and put aside his feminine clothes. In certain circumstances this may be difficult for the boy or alternatively he may accept the masculine rôle almost too thoroughly and everything feminine may become taboo. Nevertheless he cannot alter his nature completely. There remains in him his feminine side, and if this be repressed in favour of masculinity, his anima may appear in irrational moods, in peevishness or bad temper, and not infrequently in sexual deviation, often associated with immature emotional development. All these irregularities are disturbances of the normal operation of the feminine side of men. When understood in this way they become comprehensible as symptoms due to repression of a part of himself. In other words, such manifestations are an unconscious effort to bring about self-regulation through compensation.

Jung considered this attempt at compensation was of special importance in the second half of life, that is from about the age of thirty-six onward. During the first part of life the man is making his way and developing his career, concerned with the family and other interests which demand conscious rational adaptation. He thinks clearly and acts without effort. He is unaware that his anima exists because it finds easy and natural expression in friendships with girls. This is healthy in adolescence and in the twenties, but not if it continues year after year, as it often does. Such projections can, of course, lead to disaster, and the man may learn by bitter experience that he cannot disregard parts of his normal make-up without penalty. Jung writes: "In dealing with the shadow or anima it is not sufficient just to know about these concepts and to reflect on them. Nor can we ever experience their content by feeling our way into them or by appropriating other people's feelings. It is no use at all to learn a list of archetypes by heart. . . . The anima no longer crosses our path as a goddess, but, it may be, as an intimately personal misadventure, or perhaps as our best venture. When, for instance, a highly esteemed professor in his seventies abandons his family and runs off with a young red-headed actress, we know that the gods have claimed another victim. This is how daemonic power reveals itself to us. Until not so long ago it would have been an easy matter to do away with the young woman as a witch."[74]

"It is often tragic," says Jung, "to see how blatantly a man bungles his own life and the lives of others yet remains totally incapable of seeing how much the whole tragedy originates in himself, and how he continually feeds it and keeps it going."[75]

"Woman, with her very dissimilar psychology, is and always has been a source of information about things for which a man has no eyes. She can be his inspiration; her intuitive capacity, often superior to man's . . . can show him ways which his own, less personally accented feeling, would never have discovered. . . . Here without a doubt is one of the main sources for the feminine quality of the soul. No man is so entirely masculine that he has nothing feminine in him . . . there is no human experience, nor would experience be possible at all, without the intervention of a subjective aptitude. . . . Thus the whole nature of man presupposes woman, both physically and spiritually. His system is tuned in to woman from the start, just as it is prepared for a quite definite world where there is water, light, air, salt, carbohydrates, etc. . . . an inherited collective image of woman exists in a man's un-conscious."[76]

Woman completes, fulfils man. On the physical side also there is an analogous situation, for physically each sex seems to complement the other. In his body every man carries the vestigial characteristics of the woman (homo-logues), for example, vestigial breasts corresponding in type and structure to the female breast. So also with the woman who carries homologues of the man, such as the clitoris which corresponds with the penis.

Psychologically and physically the concept of the anima (and animus) is reminiscent of Plato's well-known story or myth, that originally the human being was round like a ball, signifying wholeness, and androgynous—that is, the characteristics of both sexes were united. These strange beings had four feet, four hands, one neck and two faces. Everything was double. Possessed of enormous power these male-female beings attempted to assault the gods and Zeus split each into two individual parts. Since then, the striving to be reunited is expressed in the longing of each sex for the other so that, as in the former state, they may be one.

That the psychology of men and that of women differ can hardly be questioned. Jung's postulate seems to offer a reasonable basis in explaining the psychological distinctiveness of each. This distinctiveness, as part of the natural order of life, has been taken for granted almost everywhere—except perhaps in certain areas of psychological thought. Literature provides many examples of the compulsive drive of the man towards completeness by marrying a certain woman upon whom he has pro-jected his anima. An example appears in Hardy's novel,

The Well Beloved, which was published while Jung was still a student. Jung first saw the book many years after his work on the *anima* and *animus* had been published. In the novel Hardy traces the career of a man who fell in love at first sight with a girl. He did not meet her again for a considerable time, yet he remained convinced that the success and fulfilment of his life lay in marrying this girl. Dante, from what we know of his life, had much the same experience when he met Beatrice when she was eight years and four months old and he was nearly nine.

Jung considered Rider Haggard's *She* gave an interesting and accurate description of the "anima type" of woman. "The so-called 'sphinx-like' character is an indispensable part of their equipment, also an equivocalness, an intriguing elusiveness—not an indefinite blur that offers nothing, but an indefiniteness that seems full of promises, like the speaking silence of a Mona Lisa. A woman of this kind is both old and young, mother and daughter, of more than doubtful chastity, childlike and yet endowed with a naïve cunning that is extremely disarming to men."[77]

When a girl happens to be the "anima type" or, as it is sometimes put in popular language, "all-the-world's-sweetheart" she is likely to be annoyed when a man projects his anima-image upon her and insists that she is what he thinks she must be. She wants to be recognised for what she is or thinks she is, and she may find the man's attentions boring and entirely stupid. On the other hand, as the relation of the two is also on a conscious level, and as each carries, or may carry, the projections of the other, it is possible that they may form a satisfactory friendship leading to a happy marriage. Unless the man had, in the first instance, projected his anima upon the woman, the friendship might never have started. It should be remembered that the anima is an autonomous complex and is not set in movement by the conscious intentions of the man. It just "happens" that he projects his anima, that is his image and ideals of womanhood, on a particular woman. As the friendship develops her other qualities (and his) will become apparent. Consequently "falling-in-love"—whatever meaning we attach to this indefinite state of affairs—may well be a compound of projection and conscious appreciation of the qualities of the other person. In passing it may be remarked that many marriages continue to be successful when one or both partners retain their projections; they remain happily unconscious. It is not essential to insist that all projections should be dissolved "into the light of common day".

Dissolution of projections, in individual relations with the opposite sex, often happens, but this is far from invariable. Often enough an intelligent man behaves sensibly and correctly in all situations in life—with the exception of contacts with the other sex. Yet his life may be interrupted, marred, by passionate episodes in which he is absolutely certain that he must establish the closest possible friendship with a particular woman. That the same thing has happened in the past is no deterrent. He may agree that two or perhaps three marriages have been preceded by such an infatuation, and that the present friendship, to the uninvolved outsider, is a replica of others which did not last. When strong emotion dominates, common sense is powerless.

It is not unusual to find that men, having psychological treatment and using painting to make clearer their dreams or other inner thoughts, produce a picture, or a series of pictures, of an unknown woman that cannot be identified with any actual woman. Usually the eyes are veiled or the face averted. This happens again and again with men who have never heard of Jung or his concept of the anima. Such experiences support his contention: "Every man carries within him the eternal image of woman . . . an imprint or 'archetype' of all the ancestral experiences of the female, a deposit, as it were, of all the impressions ever made by woman—in short, an inherited system of psychic adaptation."[78]

"The anima," says Jung, "is presumably a psychic representation of the minority of female genes in a man's body. This is all the more probable since the same figure is not to be found in the imagery of a woman's unconscious. There is a corresponding figure, however, that plays an equivalent rôle, yet it is not a woman's image but a man's. This masculine figure in a woman's psychology has been termed the 'animus' . One of the most typical manifestations of both figures is what has long been called 'animosity' . The anima causes illogical moods, and the animus produces irritating platitudes and unreasonable opinions. Both are frequent dream-figures. As a rule they personify the unconscious and give it its peculiarly disagreeable or irritating character. The unconscious in itself has no such negative qualities. They appear only when it is personified by these figures and when they begin to influence consciousness. Being only partial personalities, they have the character either of an inferior woman or of an inferior man—hence their irritating effect. A man experiencing this influence will be subject to unaccountable moods, and a woman will be argumentative and produce opinions that are beside the mark."[79]

Alongside this we must place another statement of Jung's: "Although to begin with, we meet the anima and animus mostly in their negative and unwelcome form, they are very far from being only a species of bad spirit. They have . . . an equally positive aspect . . . they have formed since olden times, the archetypal basis of all masculine and feminine divinities and therefore merit special attention. They therefore represent a supreme pair of opposites . . . because of the mutual attraction between them, giving promise of union and actually making it possible."[80]

"When the anima is recognised and integrated a change of attitude occurs toward the feminine generally . . . for life is founded on the harmonious interplay of masculine and feminine forces, within the individual human being as well as without. Bringing these opposites into union is one of the most important tasks of present-day psychotherapy."[81]

THE ANIMUS

Since the girl and the boy as members of the same family have a similar environment, it is to be expected that the girl's image of the other sex will come to be formed, *mutatis mutandis*, on the same framework as the boy's. We have then the girl's experience of her father, who becomes an all-important image in her mind. Upon this background she will probably build her ideas about men. He is the first man she meets and, by choice or involuntarily, he becomes the model or standard by which she assesses men. Supplementary to this source of the masculine side of herself, there is the cumulative impression from conversations she hears about men—conversations in the home, her mother's remarks, gossip from girls at school, and her own experiences. All these add to, but do not displace, the image of her father. There is also the inherited image of man in the woman's un- conscious. Just as the boy is born already fitted and adapted to the other sex, so the girl arrives equipped with a similar attitude towards men. Her life can be fulfilled through men or more probably through one man. For this masculine element in the woman, Jung employed the term *animus*. His description of the animus is an original contribution of practical importance to the psychology of women.

Possibly with the majority of women the unconscious masculine elements in her personality are harmoniously blended with other attributes and so contribute to healthy living. Like other qualities, the individual girl or woman has no option about having an animus; it is part of her normal endowment. However, the animus is not always happily blended.

One of the simplest ways of observing the presence of an unhealthy animus is by noting how the girl gets on with other people. If her friendships seem to be normal and natural, and particularly if she meets the other sex spontaneously and happily, all may be well. On the other hand, as she grows up, perhaps when she goes to the university or takes an appointment, she may slowly but surely build up a reputation amongst her contemporaries for being "difficult". They may have noticed her inability to appreciate the feelings of others, although perhaps they are unable to put it quite so simply as this. People will be affronted by her, particularly men, and she will be astonished that they are upset at her remarks because surely she was entirely reasonable. If not, why didn't they say so? For her the matter may end there. Probably her remarks were reasonable; but the feelings of other people do not depend only on reason. If she has never noticed these oft-repeated incidents—and this is likely—she will make enemies and lose her men and women friends.

Let us suppose her father—an important source of the animus—was a failure *qua* father—supposing he left his wife and went off with someone else. Perhaps the marriage continued, but he was morose and silent, got on badly with her mother or in some other way there was constraint between them or times when they did not speak to one another. These experiences affect her image of her father, and as he is the prototype of men for her, the influence will persist; unwittingly she will tend to meet all men with reservations—felt by them, though perhaps not by her. She might be unaware of any reservation and disown such an idea; nevertheless she will be inclined to upset men and she may not notice that she is doing so. She does not want to offend them and her intentions may be admirable. But should a man contradict her, however politely, or question her *bona fides*, he will be "shot down" instantly, to his surprise. Her reaction seems disproportioned. This is because without realising it she is perpetually on the defensive, and so exonerates herself, whatever the cost. Or if this is impossible she will find a scapegoat. This sort of thing may occur again and again and yet make no impression on her. Often she is generous to a fault and helps those who ask for her co-operation. She finds it easier to give than to receive. She makes the sad mistake of undervaluing, just a little, the opinion of others. It may be difficult to tell her anything; either she knows it already, or if she does not, she is likely to indicate that it is of no importance anyhow.

Alternatively, should her father have been a success *qua* father, automatically he becomes a trusted source of affection and security. His daughter may then idealise him, feel she is owned by him, that she knows and understands him better than anyone else. This happens all the more easily should her mother be dead; but the presence of her mother does not necessarily rule it out. A girl's close link with her father is often broken, to her distress: he may remarry or he may go and live elsewhere. But the effect of the early identification with him remains and she may find it impossible ever to establish a close bond with another man. Probably this will be against her conscious wishes; yet she is unable to give herself, even in marriage: she always keeps back something, guided by an unconscious motive that she must never entrust herself to another man. This can lead to homosexual attachments which may or may not be accompanied by physical manifestations.

It is healthy for women to have opinions, and they would be very dull without them; but the woman with an animus problem may become opinionated, that is, her opinions may be thrust upon other people. As expressed, her opinions may be sensible and original. Nevertheless the hidden motive for putting them forward is usually to score points. This activates the anima in a man and he will feel indignant beyond the needs of the situation. If he knows nothing about feminine psychology he will argue with the woman, little knowing that her tendency will be to argue for the sake of argument, not to discover the truth. She will achieve trivial verbal successes and before very long the successes themselves pave the way for defeat. Unfortunately for her she does not recognise her defeats and the same pattern is repeated. Naturally the activity of the animus will be affected by the woman's functional type (p. 54) and her natural gifts. She may be highly intelligent with brilliant ideas, and these may be focused upon some project which succeeds for a time and then falters. Nothing seems to get built up around her. There is strife without and conflict within, and as she gets older she may find herself too much alone, her friends having disappeared.

An illusion many women have to overcome, if they are to be healthy, is that they are being attacked. They behave as though the world at large was hostile. Should they be endowed with charm and beauty, this can be used almost as a means of keeping men at bay. Men will be attracted by a girl's beauty, but they will not see anything else, and she will enjoy their admiration. Nevertheless their appreciation is not reciprocated and she may look on her physical attractiveness as a weapon. Adulation is easily accepted; she needs praise for everything she does; without it she feels lost. Of course there are faults on both sides, and it is not always easy for a girl to show her feelings.

Perhaps this picture will seem over-drawn, and it does not apply to every woman; nor are the regrettable features of the animus evident every day of the week. For long periods there may be happy contacts. Nevertheless it is a true picture of the psychology of many women who hurt and alienate their friends, and blindly ruin what is precious in their personal life. They are badly adjusted emotionally and tend to blame others for their failures.

In analytical treatment it is difficult, sometimes impossible, to make the concept of the animus clear to a woman in whom the masculine elements in her personality are not harmoniously blended (see p. 129). She is her own worst enemy. Her autonomous animus is always on the defensive, impelled by a strong desire to be right and to get in first, and so to avoid a situation where she might be rejected. Of course this exaggeration of the animus is a burden to the woman. But its recognition is the means by which she can achieve her full development. It can be a great practical help to a woman who wants to know how the animus operates, to get her to write down her dreams and to use every means in her power, such as painting pictures or modelling, to give shape and form to the animus quality which is disturbing her life. So long as she is unaware of its existence it acts autonomously and destructively. Such a woman behaves as though she is afraid of losing control, and no situation in which her feelings are involved is allowed to develop naturally. She interrupts or in some unpredictable way makes others feel they have missed the point.

If she is to play her part happily and in harmony with others she must become more conscious of the masculine features in her personality. These are over-prominent and they obscure her much more important feminine qualities. A woman requires courage and patience to undertake self-examination or to accept the well-meant comments of others. She must learn that her true strength lies in sympathetic recognition of the feelings of others. When this is accomplished the woman carries out her true rôle: she keeps the group, the family, together. Being less concerned with personal achievements, she is more in touch with the inner world of the unconscious. Remembering that the animus is a figure in the collective unconscious, it will be important for her to pay attention to her dreams. From them she should expect to learn and, in consequence, to be able to make the necessary compensatory adjustments. Also there will be a gain in discovering how she may acquire a less personal—that is a more impersonal—outlook in her efforts to be a woman. With widening consciousness the energy wasted in petty encounters may be used to put her in touch with the external world. But first she must establish links with the unconscious, the inner world, and so grow beyond the unsatisfying attempts to establish herself by what Jung calls "the extraversion of the animus". "Instead of the woman merely associating opinions with external situations—situations which she ought to think about consciously—the animus as an associative function should be directed inwards where it could associate the contents of the unconscious . . . the woman must learn to criticize and hold her opinions at a distance; not in order to repress them, but by investigating their origins, to penetrate more deeply into the background . . . the inner masculine side of the woman brings forth creative seeds which have the power to fertilize the feminine side of the man."[82]

Many women, through analysis, have seen the negative effects of their animus tendencies and have corrected them. This makes a striking difference in their personal life: they get on more easily with other people on a conscious level—an essential step in understanding the impersonal, archetypal material of life. They are at peace with themselves and, inevitably, impart an atmosphere of quiet confidence. The positive qualities of the animus will be noted in dreams, and these should be discussed simply and clearly, avoiding abstraction, so that the woman has a chance to realise in what way she can do justice to herself. Within her grasp is the possibility of forming a bridge between her conscious life and unconscious background, which, it should be remembered, works autonomously. This is never easy in practice; but with good-will it can be done. She must do most of the work by valuing her unconscious—that is, by noting dreams, by active imagination and painting, and in other ways. By these means her life will develop and begin to lose its asperities; she becomes prepared to receive as well as to give.

Men are quickly aware of the woman whose animus is *not* overdeveloped. She has the indefinable quality known as charm; she is interested in the man, enjoys hearing what he has got to say, and her enjoyment is genuine. Such a woman would fit into the "world's lover" group; but it should be noted that she, too, has an animus, although it is not pathologically prominent. Nevertheless it is there, and gives her an immediate affinity with men, as though she knew something about them already. Observation shows that women of this kind tend to get on well with everyone because they are seldom on the defensive, they feel no desire to score points, and they are not shattered by making a mistake.

Jung's description of the anima and animus was based on prolonged observation of what was going on in the unconscious of men and of women. His evaluation of the unconscious is highly practical, not at all visionary, and it makes it possible to understand numerous all too human situations.

6

THE WIDENING
CIRCLE OF JUNG'S THOUGHT

When Jung joined the staff of the Burghölzli Hospital in December 1900 it marked a turning point in his career. To leave Basel for Zürich meant more than a change of surroundings to take up new work. "In Basel," writes Jung, "I was stamped for all time as the son of the Reverend Paul Jung and the grandson of Professor Carl Gustav Jung (Professor of Medicine at the University). I was an intellectual and belonged to a definite social set. I felt resistances against this, for I could not and would not let myself be classified."[83] He was unknown in Zürich when he took his first appointment in a mental hospital. Yet the fates ordained that in Zürich, and in Küsnacht on the Zürich Lake, he was to live his life and become a world figure in psychiatric thought.

HYPNOTISM

At the Burghölzli he had responsibility for patients and their treatment and, like his colleagues, he undertook research. Soon he began to give lectures and demonstrations for medical students who attended the practice of the hospital. This suited him exactly; he was launched on the career of his choice and his hope and ambition was to dissipate some of the mystery surrounding mental illness and to discover what was going on in the minds of patients with mental disturbances.

Speaking broadly there were two groups of patients: first, the severely disturbed, suffering from psychosis, many of whom were incurable. Their treatment was limited to custodial care and attention to physical health. Secondly there were those with less severe illness, with symptoms of morbid anxiety, phobias, obsessions, and other forms of neurosis, some psychopaths, and some with sexual deviations. An effort was made to give active treatment to the second group, although at that time no one knew what had brought on the illness or what the symptoms meant. They were helped, in the hospital and in the out-patient clinic, by simple psychotherapy in the form of good advice, encouragement, and perhaps sedation. Jung learnt a lot from talking with these patients. Many of them improved, no doubt because of the encouragement and support they received.

In his early years at the Burghölzli Jung spent some months, in 1902, doing post-graduate study in Paris at the Salpêtrière Hospital under Professor Pierre Janet, whose original work on hysteria and other neuroses impressed him. Janet had used hypnosis extensively, and so had several well-known psychiatrists in Switzerland. Consequently in his lectures to students at that time Jung gave a prominent place to hypnotism, and, as happens today, the subject aroused interest amongst the students. The use of hypnosis and group hypnosis was well established in the Burghölzli when Jung went there; Eugen Bleuler's predecessor, Professor August Forel, had introduced hypnotic treatment.

Rather to his surprise, Jung found no difficulty in inducing hypnosis and he had plenty of opportunities to use it. Treatment should depend on the views of the therapist about the cause or significance of the symptoms, but at this stage he had no strong opinion about causation; he was a beginner and had an open mind. Nevertheless he made it a rule to go into the history of his patients, as far as possible, to find out what their symptoms meant. If a patient had paralysis of a leg, without any physical impairment, he would try to find out when the symptom had first appeared and what the patient's state of mind had been at the time: why did the illness take that form? why a paralysed leg? Such a choice of symptom could not be mere chance.

In those days many doctors were convinced that "nerves" (i.e. neurosis) was due to "imagination", and they welcomed any method that might dispose of the silly ideas the patient had got into his head. On the whole hypnotic treatment was popular: patients thought there was something wonderful about it, and the doctors got a lot of kudos; frequently it produced immediate, if short-lived, relief of symptoms. But Jung was sceptical. He found the number of cures disappointingly small. It was an uncertain method, and many patients could not be hypnotised. He was told by an older member of the staff that in the past most of the patients having group hypnosis sat still with their eyes closed and pretended they were hypnotized, thinking that Professor Forel would be annoyed if they had not gone into a trance.

So far as investigation went, on which treatment could be based, Jung found individual and group hypnosis more and more unsatisfactory. At times he got fairly good symptomatic results without being any the wiser about the origin of the illness. Working in the dark did not suit him. In addition, he found that patients often became dependent on him and insisted on looking upon him as a wizard. This puzzled him; but gradually he came to understand: the induction of hypnosis depended on suggestion, and the patient, having been put in a trance and relieved of some symptom, not unnaturally assumed he possessed some special "power" or "gift". To Jung this was altogether distasteful, and in consequence of these experiences and the superficial nature of hypnotism he gave it up. To have produced a "cure", and yet to have no idea how it happened, did not appeal to him.

THE COMPLEX IN TREATMENT

From his word association experiments, already mentioned (p. 25), Jung demonstrated the autonomous nature of the unconscious, seen in the formation of complexes and the effect of these in delayed reaction time, usually with physiological accompaniments. This was a significant finding, and Jung and his colleagues were enthusiastic. Since the results of the test had a direct bearing on the treatment of patients, hopes rose that they might discover the origin of symptoms and so open the way to cure.

As a "complex-indicator" the word association method was most useful in treatment as it focused attention on events or ideas in the patient's mind of which he, as well as the doctor, was ignorant. Conversations would follow with the aim of making the hidden matter accessible to conscious direction. With this method Jung could show patients how the recording indicated, beyond question, their delayed reaction to a particular stimulus word, and how it had affected the breathing and caused the heart to beat faster, as well as slowing up their verbal response. Patients had not noticed the delay in their reply, and they were quite unable to explain the altered breathing or increased heart-beat. Obviously their picture of themselves was incomplete. Hidden emotion showed up plainly on the chart so that the doctor began his enquiries with confidence. Such clues were always followed up, and constantly it was found that some past event was still affecting the patient and causing symptoms, although he might have no recollection of the episode. This was real progress: the circle had widened.

Jung's application of the word association test was a great achievement. Doctors from overseas visited Zürich to learn the method and it became well known and widely used. Later Jung gave a series of lectures on the subject in the United States. It seemed that there was a bright future for this technique. It was an illusion to think, as many did, that consciousness was synonymous with our total personality. Quite conclusively the tests showed that the personality was "bigger" than consciousness. Consciousness has marked limits, for instance, in maintaining concentration. As the word association test revealed, the unconscious plays a decisive rôle. In applying the tests Jung observed movements of the hands and feet, coughing, laughing, etc., as well as the reaction time. When a subject replied with the same word again and again to a number of stimulus words, he looked into this carefully. That these reactions were all beyond the control of the will was a most impressive discovery. One group of tests was made with families, and it was found that the type of association and reaction was to a remarkable extent parallel amongst certain members of a family, such as two brothers, or a mother and a child. This pointed to the presence of identification (p. 25).

Unfortunately the test was not faultless. It had numerous drawbacks: that the doctor was using a stop-watch and concentrating upon it, and then marking the chart, introduced a mechanical element which interfered with the doctor-patient relation. During the test the patient, inevitably, took second place. For these reasons, amongst others, Jung came to use the test less and less. Yet in spite of its limitations it had been an invaluable research instrument and he continued to use the tests for some years, mainly for diagnostic purposes, in conjunction with other methods of treatment. More than anything else it led the way to his later work. "It was these association studies," writes Jung, "which later, in 1909, procured me my invitation to Clark University; I was asked to lecture on my work. Simultaneously, and independently of me, Freud was invited."[84] As we have seen, it was as a result of test findings pointing to repression, that Jung came to know Freud (p. 34).

Following his contact with Freud, Jung's methods in treatment began to widen and he paid more and more attention to the dreams of patients. Freud's psychoanalysis was included in his programme of lectures to students.

In these early days Jung tried various methods; but he always avoided a rigid psychotherapeutic technique. Each patient must be treated as an individual: each had his own problem, each his motives; no two were identical. Jung entered fully into the treatment, and by sitting facing his patient, his participation was obvious to the patient as well. To his way of thinking a couch was a barrier, and interrupted the co-operation of two people—the patient and the analyst. His individual flexible method in treatment was taking shape, more by what he did not do than by any novel additions. Any "technique", such as the word association test, or the artificiality of the patient lying on a couch, was, to Jung, a hindrance rather than a help.

THE PSYCHOLOGY OF THE UNCONSCIOUS

Concurrently his research into the meaning of symptoms, and more important still, into the meaning of the symbols in the dreams recounted in treatment, went on. An example of this was the significant conclusion he reached about a particularly difficult type of patient he often encountered: "I realized that I could not treat latent psychoses if I did not understand their symbolism. It was then that I began to study mythology."[85] This gives us a glimpse of how Jung's circle of thought was constantly widening. From his knowledge of mythology he came to see a connecting link "between ancient mythology and the psychology of primitives, and this led me to an intensive study of the latter". About the same time a senior colleague asked him to read a document containing the fantasies of a young American woman. This amazed him. "I was immediately struck by the mythological character of the fantasies. They operated like a catalyst upon the stored-up and still disorderly ideas within me. Gradually, there formed out of them, and out of the knowledge of myths I had acquired, my book *The Psychology of the Unconscious.*"[86] His work with Freud came to an end with the publication of this book (p. 40). Jung felt very much alone. He had many friends in the psychoanalytical movement and he regretted breaking these ties. There was also the by no means unimportant fact that the medical profession in Zürich and elsewhere identified him with Freud's movement, and so, for a time, he was not asked to see their patients. This, however, was of little moment, for before long he had almost too many patients coming to him from overseas. The outcome of greatest value was that he had more time to follow up his own lines of reading, research and thinking. This he did without sparing himself.

So far as the treatment of patients was concerned he retained an open mind, and he was prepared to alter his own procedure at any time should he find reasons for so doing. He writes: "It would be an unpardonable error to overlook the element of truth in both the Freudian and the Adlerian viewpoints, but it would be no less unpardonable to take either of them as the sole truth. . . . There are in fact some cases which by and large can best be described and explained by the one theory, and some by the other. . . . It would certainly never have occurred to me to depart from Freud's path had I not stumbled upon facts which forced me into modifications. And the same is true of my relation to the Adlerian viewpoint."[87]

In writing this Jung had in mind the limitations imposed on thought by Freud's emphasis on the aberrations of the sexual libido in infancy as the causative factor in all neurosis; and likewise, the Adlerian insistence upon the universal validity of his theory that a neurosis is a system of subterfuges through which one is exonerated from responsibility for the demands of life, and gains power over those in the environment.

Freud sought an explanation for neurosis in past events, whereas Adler saw the neurosis as an arrangement indicating design and purpose to control the future and secure supremacy.

Looking at these two theories of neurosis Jung took a different line: "The symptoms of neurosis are not simply the effects of long past causes, whether 'infantile sexuality' or the infantile urge to power; they are also attempts at a new synthesis of life—unsuccessful attempts, let it be added in the same breath, yet attempts nevertheless with a core of value and meaning."[88]

THE CURRENT PROBLEM

Jung's main conclusion, at this stage, was that the symptom, in treatment, was not exclusively a heritage, a carry over, from the past, nor an effort to gain control over future eventualities, but a failure to cope with the situation in existence at the present moment. This became a main point in treatment in Analytical Psychology. Dream-analysis was becoming central in treatment, and this meant a careful, and often prolonged anamnesis, a recalling to mind of events in childhood, such as the attitude towards each parent, to brothers and sisters and others in the environment of infancy and childhood, incidents at home and in school life, and so on. Without this history, dreams would be unintelligible, and so would the dreamer's present situation and his future plans (p. 84). But important though this history was, it did not explain why the break-down took place now. If the cause lay exclusively in the past, why had there been no sign of a break-down earlier? In the dream past events might appear; but why did they appear at that time? It could only mean that in the dream the past and the present met. Likewise the so-called anticipatory dream placed the centre of activity in the present. A nervous break-down occurs in the present and must be dealt with in the present, not in the past, not in the future. Jung was convinced that the events of the current period in a patient's life and thought were significant in relation to his illness.

Even during their period of co-operation Jung did not follow Freud's practice of getting his patients to lie on a couch during treatment sessions. Lying relaxed on a couch made it possible to pursue the basic rule of psycho-analysis, that is free-association, the patient speaking without emendation of everything that comes into his mind, just as it comes.

Jung could not accept this technique and in fact disapproved of it, preferring *amplification* (p. 100), a form of association differing from free-association in an important way: should a patient be asked to give his association upon a feature in a dream, he confined his remarks to that feature and did not let his thoughts wander fancy-free. During the analytical session Jung and his patient met on equal terms, and the interview, in Jung's words, "should resemble a social occasion with mutual conversational exchange and if the person has a neurosis then that also would be discussed, but in the same way as other occurrences". He learned, he went on, never to start an interview, beyond a few pleasantries—How are you?—and then wait for the patient. His reason was that we don't know what is there. "Between the patient and myself," he remarked, "lie the instincts, the archetypes, the unconscious. So I prefer to wait and let the patient make a start."

In Jung's opinion a formal technique, such as free-association, brought a suggestive element into the interview; how could it be otherwise? Lying on a couch conveys a suggestion of illness. Also it was used in the technique of hypnotism where the patient lost the initiative and depended on the hypnotist. To Jung this kind of procedure seemed the antithesis of an interchange of conversation.

An interview with Jung often surprised patients who had seen other psychiatrists. It was completely informal; he rarely took notes. He asked questions but he did not dominate the interview. All the time Jung had in mind the important question: how does this situation appear from the other side, from the unconscious? His manner was informal yet there was no trace of casualness. What his patient had to say interested him; he did not guide the conversation; he let it take its course, knowing that what cropped up was relevant. It was a conversation and not a monologue. As the activity of the unconscious is evident in ordinary conversation, for example, through memory, so it is in an interview with a patient, and Jung relied on it. Usually he would enquire about recent dreams during the first interview, that is, the initial dream (p. 86). He would also ask about the patient's everyday life, occupation, family situation, general health and in particular the current situation. Generally an interview with Jung would last about an hour and arrangements would be made for further meetings if treatment was to be undertaken.

Jung was often asked by patients to explain what had happened during an interview, for it did affect them. Had he hypnotized them, or what? Of course he told them that there was no question of hypnosis. At the same time it was obvious that the interview contained more than an ordinary conversation: it was private, and the patient talked only about himself and Jung gave him his complete attention. Sometimes the patient enquired when "treatment" was going to begin. This was understandable; the patient was in an unfamiliar situation with a strange doctor and wondered what he was going to do.

If treatment continues, as in analysis, the response to the situation of both patient and doctor will come to the fore, as it ought to do. When confidential and secret matters are discussed between two people, each will have an effect on the other. There is no escaping this. It occurs between a patient and a doctor engaged in general practice; between a clergyman and someone consulting him on personal matters; between a solicitor and his client, when personal matters are relevant. It is bound to be a feature—and a very important feature—of interchanges between a psychiatrist and a patient having psychotherapy or analysis. In the latter the unconscious motives are surveyed, as in dream-analysis, so that while the interview has resemblances to other private consultations, it has the important difference that the analyst, having accepted the patient for treatment, cannot, like the solicitor, for example, shake hands with his patient and wish him (or her) good-bye. Presuming the co-operation of the patient, he must continue with the treatment. In this situation each plays a part, and each must react in some way to the other. Freud was the first to observe that the patient is prone to attribute thoughts and emotions, friendly or hostile, to the analyst which do not properly belong to him, but have their origin in his own childhood experience with his parents. He coined the term *transference* to describe what was taking place. Jung saw the importance of this, and later he gave the term *transference* a wider meaning as he considered that any thoughts or feelings might be transferred and not only those from the child-parent relation.

TRANSFERENCE IN THE DOCTOR-PATIENT RELATION

In his early professional life Jung was aware that the meeting between a patient and an analyst, during treatment, was liable to be complicated by the phenomenon of transference. Thus patients might insist that the analyst was unusually clever; that he understood them perfectly, and in other ways indicate appreciation of his personality. For the analyst this made matters run smoothly; there was no tiresome questioning or irritation. This wonderfully co-operative atmosphere did not always last. Bit by bit the atmosphere might cloud, statements would be questioned, appointments might be missed and, in general, co-operation became less harmonious. When this was first observed it was not understood—perhaps it is not yet fully understood.

This direction of feelings and thoughts towards or upon another person is well described as transference, which means to carry over something from one place, or as in analysis, from one person, to another. Transference is a form of projection, and like all projections it is unconscious.

As transference is spontaneous and unsought it cannot be disposed of by explaining the process of projection. Projection is only known through its effects; it "happens" unconsciously; as the projection is unconscious, so also are the contents. When a projection becomes recognised by the person who "sent" it, it may disappear because it is understood. But bringing about this dissolution of the projection can be a difficult matter. Jung's opinion about transference varied. In 1942 he wrote: "I am not of the opinion that the transference to the doctor is a regular phenomenon indispensable to the success of treatment. Transference is projection, and projection is either there or not there. But it is not *necessary*. . . . The absence of projections to the doctor may in fact considerably facilitate the treatment, because the real personal values can then come more clearly to the forefront."[89] In a later work, *Psychology of the Transference*,[90] an editorial note points out that in this volume we have the only authoritative statement from Jung's pen of the way in which the individuation process (p. 171) expresses itself in the transference. In a foreword Jung says that when lengthy psychological treatment is needed, its success or failure is bound up with the phenomenon of the transference. But cases vary: at times the appearance of transference indicates a beneficial change in the course of treatment; but it can be "a hindrance and an aggravation, if not a change for the worse, and in a third it is relatively unimportant . . . like those medicines which are a panacea for one and pure poison for another".

Jung considered the transference as a critical

phenomenon and that its absence should always be noted, for it may be as significant as its presence. In *Psychology of the Transference*, Jung describes and explains the "classical" form of transference. Difficult problems arise in such an investigation and its "provisional character" is emphasized. The book was written for the guidance of the experienced psychotherapist, already familiar with his earlier work, including his *Psychology and Alchemy*. Such readers "will know what close connections exist between alchemy and those phenomena which must, for practical reasons, be considered in the psychology of the unconscious".[91] Jung, of course, was interested only in the philosophical aspects of alchemy and not at all in the activities of the alchemists who wanted to find a short-cut to wealth by turning base metals into gold. Alchemy flourished from pre-Christian times till the seventeenth century, so naturally it took many forms.

As the present book is written for the information of non-experts it must be added that Jung attached importance to the fact that the study of alchemy provided "a point outside our own time from which to come to a right understanding and appreciation of a contemporary psychological problem".[92]

Later we read, "The main problem of medical psychotherapy is the *transference*. . . ."[93]

An impersonal attitude on the part of the analyst is out of the question in treatment; he is *in* the treatment and so is bound to be affected by it. Two influences are at work: that of the patient upon him, and his own unconscious reaction to the situation. "The intelligent psychotherapist," writes Jung, "has known for years that any complicated treatment is an individual, dialectical process, in which the doctor, as a person, participates just as must as the patient."[94] In other words, the doctor and the patient engage in a dialectical interchange that is a critical examination of the subject matter produced by the patient. No longer is the doctor the source of all information, the superior judge. He is a participant in the process and is as much involved as the patient. In such a relation, rapport, that is, mutual confidence is essential, and without it the treatment cannot progress.

That such a bond or link springs up between doctor and patient is a fact of observation. Subjective contents of any kind may be projected. As projection is unconscious it is non-volitional, and consequently cannot be demanded; nor can it be refused. The therapist has no option about transference. If he is properly trained he will realise what is happening and will accept responsibility for enlightening his patient. Jung always insisted that before a psychiatrist undertook the treatment of patients he must himself have been analysed. This proposition, made by Jung and supported by Freud at one of the early psychoanalytical conferences, has been widely accepted. Therefore the analyst knows, or ought to know, what is involved in the "transference situation".

Transference projections will affect the analyst, and, to quote Jung: "If he does not see that, he is too aloof and then he talks beside the mark. It is even his duty to accept the emotions of the patient and to mirror them. That is the reason why I reject the idea of putting the patient upon a sofa and sitting behind him. I put my patients in front of me and I talk to them as one natural human being to another."[95]

As a rule the transference comes unexpectedly. It may

be spontaneous, or the seeds of it may be sown before doctor and patient have met through the patient having heard of the doctor, or having read something he has written. When the personalities of the patient and of the analyst are in marked contrast, it may be nearly impossible to find a basis for co-operative treatment. In such circumstances a strong positive transference may appear, unsought, to bridge the gap, to compensate for the absence of rapport.

As in life the course of human association is liable to fluctuate, so in analysis the transference is not always on the same emotional level. It can alter, sometimes in a moment, from a positive transference when everything is going smoothly, to negative, when nothing works easily and the patient and the doctor are at cross purposes. This is just as important as a positive transference and should not be looked on as a personal attack. Later on, when the patient has come to understand the significance of projection in the transference, there will be gratitude for the analyst's sensitive understanding at a critical juncture.

In handling the transference wisely, the analyst requires objective detachment, with some "understanding of the heart", particularly during interviews when the emotional atmosphere is a living reality. In this connection the reader is reminded that while Jung was specially interested in the activity of the unconscious as a source of creative activity, he was alive to the importance of conscious activity. Transference is an expression of the feeling function, which may be central and all-pervading. Thinking, as a function, is at a discount. This brief reference to Jung's typology may be sufficient to show that the conscious and unconscious, as opposites, are always involved in a transference situation. It was pointed out

(p. 53) that Jung's typology and his description of extra-version and introversion must be looked at alongside his views on the phenomena of the unconscious. It goes without saying that the converse is true—the unconscious can be understood only when the conscious attitude of mind is also in the picture. Here again is an example of the widening circle of Jung's thought. But, it may be asked, what happens eventually to the transference bond? First of all the projections must be understood by the patient; the energy involved belongs to the patient and should be restored to him. Of this Jung writes: "To the extent that the transference is projection and nothing more, it divides quite as much as it connects. But experience teaches that there is one connection in the transference which does not break off with the severance of the projection. That is because there is an extremely important instinctive factor behind it: the kinship libido."[96]

Kinship libido (energy) is comparable to the invisible bonds which serve to hold the family together. In the family it is accepted as healthy that the kinship should eventually lead quite naturally to close associations in the outer world. Thus transference and kinship libido are not a terminus, but a stage in personal development. In analysis there may well be something of this feeling for those with whom co-operative work—often hard work—has been done. Yet this should be a stepping-stone to enduring connections outside the analytical situation. We can never say exactly where or what these will be. That is for the future. Beyond a certain point we cannot plan ahead, especially when feeling is prominent. It is here that the quality of the analyst is tested to the full.

In the previous chapter it was seen that dream-analysis

has a central place in the therapy of Analytical Psychology. Both doctor and patient know how true this is in resolving the complexities of the transference situation, for the dreams make a silent, but objective, comment on how matters stand. It was from his research into dreams that Jung came to formulate his theory of self-regulation (p. 91) and compensation. Likewise, it was through the investigation of dreams that he arrived at the hypothesis of the personal and collective unconscious. In the last chapter an account was given of four figures in the unconscious: persona, shadow, animus/anima—which represent aspects of the personal and impersonal qualities of the mind. The anima and animus are archetypes, but the persona represents a personal attribute, and so does the shadow except where the term is used to describe everything in the unconscious (p. 118). There are many other figures. The archetypes represent all the general human situations; any universally human mode of behaviour is an archetype. Inevitably these have taken innumerable forms, and they become perceptible as images in the mind. When obscure features occur in a dream, they may be of an archetypal or collective nature; there may be no personal associations by the method of amplification, and explanatory remarks of the analyst may not make the matter comprehensible. In such a situation Jung often advised painting and modelling, for words are not always adequate (p. 111). Active imagination can be invaluable when the ego-consciousness has gone as far as it can, and yet more is required. There are many phases in psychological treatment, including the transference situation, when it is wise to "stop trying" and let the unconscious find an outlet. From this it will be evident that Jung never clung slavishly to one method or one form of treatment. There must always be flexibility.

When two people are seriously engaged in the dialectical discussion called analysis, this amounts to a discussion between the conscious and the unconscious of each, and it is based on the assumption that there is some goal, some end in view. Requirements vary from one person to another. With some a comparatively simple explanation will suffice or the effect of confessing openly some hitherto sealed bit of experience may bring relief. For others acceptance of the unconscious message, conveyed in a dream, can open up the way. In treatment, by analysis or in some other form, it is impossible to take people beyond their natural possibilities, or what they consider to be their needs. For others, however, the early stages of self-realisation are not enough. Many of Jung's patients sought for more and followed up their analysis on their own initiative. This attitude is entirely healthy and need not be given up at the end of a period of treatment. Psychological treatment is not at all like having one's appendix removed. On the contrary, it may be a continuing means of enlightenment, not just in coping with problems, but in helping us to live complete lives. For many it is possible and desirable that knowledge of their own unconscious should be looked for by observing their dreams, or possibly by painting and modelling. No one way suits everybody.

JUNG'S INTEREST IN ALCHEMY

Anticipatory dreams, mentioned earlier (p. 89), are by no means unusual and most people have had them. Jung had many dreams of this type and for years they were a mystery to him. In one of them a new wing had been added to his house. "The unknown wing of the house was a part of my personality . . . it represented something that belonged to me but of which I was not yet conscious . . ."[97] The library, a large and attractive room, was full of wonderful manuscripts. Jung had this dream many times and could make nothing of it till he began to study alchemy. In 1926 he had another dream of a similar type and in trying to understand it he read "ponderous tomes" on religion and philosophy and some on alchemy, without enlightenment. "I regarded alchemy as something off the beaten track, rather silly. . . ."[98] A year or two later Richard Wilhelm sent him a translation of an ancient text on Chinese Alchemy entitled *The Secret of the Golden Flower*.* Reading this remarkable book aroused Jung's interest in alchemy and he began to collect the writings of alchemists. Bit by bit he acquired a large collection—probably the largest in private ownership—of sixteenth and seventeenth century alchemical texts. His knowledge of Latin, including mediaeval Latin, enabled him to read these old books. At first he thought it was a lot of rubbish, but he persisted. Working along philological lines he made a lexicon of key phrases with cross references, and very slowly he got the meaning of these obscure texts. He was thrilled by his discovery: "I had stumbled upon the historical counterpart of my psychology of the unconscious . . . when I pored over these old texts everything fell into place: the fantasy-images, the empirical material I had gathered in my practice, and the

The Secret of the Golden Flower. Translated and explained by Richard Wilhelm with a European Commentary by C. G. Jung. London: Kegan Paul, Trench, Trubner and Co. Ltd. 1932.

conclusions I had drawn from it. . . . The primordial images and the nature of the archetype took a central place in my researches, and it became clear to me that without history there can be no psychology, and certainly no psychology of the unconscious."[99]

To his surprise he found that mental energy and the importance of the opposites (p. 92) was known to the alchemists. "The problem of opposites called up by the shadow, plays a great—indeed, the decisive—role in alchemy, since it leads in the ultimate phase of the work to the union of opposites in the archetypal form of the *hieros gamos* (sacred marriage) or (alchemical) 'chymical marriage'. Here the supreme opposites, male and female . . . are melted into a unity purified of all opposition and therefore incorruptible."[100]

Pairs of opposites have been mentioned repeatedly in former chapters: the conscious and unconscious; extravert and introvert; animus and anima, and many others. They are recalled now to show that Jung's study of alchemy was not pursued merely through curiosity. Often alchemical symbolism was of the greatest help in providing a key to the symbolism he so often found in the dreams of his patients. Alchemy seemed a natural complement to much of his own analytical psychology.

Jung read the alchemical texts critically. He was not reading what someone else had to say about this strange subject: he was himself reading original manuscripts. Consequently he soon realised that there were alchemists and alchemists. Alchemy, as he understood it, was essentially a philosophical system inspired by the hope of solving one of the mysteries of life, namely, the connection between good and evil, that is, how the base aspects of life are transmuted into the noble. He knew that alongside this philosophic aspect was the other branch of alchemy which was connected with "chemistry"; how the base metal (lead) could be transmuted into the noble metal (gold).

In Chinese alchemy the notion of the opposites (The Contraries) was prominent. Such ideas and others from many sources Jung found in the ancient alchemical texts, and of course he was amazed and delighted to discover his own thought reinforced in them.

Gold represented the best symbolically, and it was supposed to have other qualities, such as producing longevity. Some alchemists made no claim to be philosophers: they were quite simply trying to make gold artificially and of course they got a bad name and alchemy was forbidden by law in some countries. Jung was aware of this trickery, and he was not thereby deflected from what he knew to be the genuine teaching of alchemy. That there were many types of alchemy in no way altered the importance he attached to what he himself had found of value in alchemistic thought. He writes: ". . . there was an 'alchymical' philosophy, the groping precursor of the most modern psychology . . . the transformation of personality through the blending and fusion of the noble with the base components, of the differentiated with the inferior functions, of the conscious with the unconscious."[101] Most of Jung's patients knew nothing of alchemy, nor was it necessary that they should. There were others who in their analysis and investigation found the concepts of alchemy of value in understanding their own psychology, and particularly in giving a suggestion in their efforts to achieve some sense of fulfilment in life.

It should be noted that Jung's conclusions were not altered in any notable way by his interest in alchemy. But with his special knowledge, the observations of the alchemists made good sense, and often they were quite penetrating, providing confirmatory evidence of the validity of his own thought and concepts, particularly as shown in everyday relationships, or even in international situations.

A symbol (p. 40) has a dynamic effect, although the reason for this may be obscure—it does not rest on a succession of logical propositions. Symbols produced spontaneously in dreams certainly played a significant part in the process of individuation (p. 171). When similar symbols were discovered in alchemy, Jung was not concerned with whether alchemy was "true" but with the fact that its study gave him many hints which were of practical importance in understanding the operation of the unconscious. We know that the alchemists projected the problem of the light and the dark, the good and the evil, upon matter. Modern man, so Jung found, is still struggling with this problem. No longer is it projected upon matter; usually it is projected upon other people, upon other nations. From this we may judge that Jung was very concerned with modern problems, which, of course, come down to problems of individuals. Such problems, on a personal or perhaps on a national level, were constantly in his mind. As an example we turn to one of his Essays, *Wotan*, published in 1936, in which he surveyed aspects of the political scene in Germany at that time. "Perhaps we can sum up this general phenomenon as *Ergriffenheit*—a state of being seized or possessed. . . . The impressive thing about the German phenomenon is that one man [Hitler] who is obviously 'possessed' has infected a whole nation. . . ."[102] Here was a contemporary event in which "the dark forces of life" confronted what we had assumed to be the enlightened modern world of reasonable economic, political and psychological factors. In other words, the conflict of opposites was at work—*enantiodromia* once more (p. 92).

Stages of human development, from babyhood to old age, raise many problems. They are not personal in infancy, for at that stage all problems are the concern of parents and others. As consciousness widens and childhood passes into adolescence, external facts may clash with subjective expectations. Sexual problems, social adaptation at school, in the university, in business, are a few of the demands each individual must encounter as he grows to maturity.

Such demands raise the all too familiar problem: to remain a child, at heart, under the protection of parents or to launch out on one's own. For the healthy such milestones are passed without distress; for others there is conflict. And this conflict may linger for years. Jung writes: ". . . the ideals, convictions, guiding ideas and attitudes which in the period of youth lead us out into life . . . we seek to perpetuate them indefinitely . . . we suppose them to be eternally valid, and make a virtue of unchangeably clinging to them. . . . The wine of youth does not always clear with advancing years; sometimes it grows turbid."[103] Such an attitude may appear in the late thirties when life should be expanding. Our bodies change, but often our outlook seems stuck in an earlier phase. There is the spring of life and also its autumn, and the movement of life calls for a corresponding development in our attitude of mind. With the onset of neurosis we generally find the inner adaptation has never even been considered. Parents, circumstances, hard luck are entirely responsible—so it is thought. Such a frame of mind is so obvious in others, though it may be invisible in ourselves. Yet these are the indications of faulty adjustment to life, as it is in the current situation. Adjustment to life means adjustment to our own development, and must involve adjustment to others.

These illustrations are a mere hint. Many others could be named, such as the application of Analytical Psychology to Religion, Education, Art and Literature, as well as to medicine. But enough has been said to show that Jungian psychology is far from being a mystical, esoteric or abstract study.

7

PRESENT AND FUTURE

Following his break with Freud Jung was uncertain about the basis of his future work. As a first step he decided he would put aside all theoretical assumptions and by his own efforts come to terms with the unconscious. Reflection on his dreams, amplification and active imagination played an important part. So also did reading and *thinking*. Systematic thinking is not so common an achievement as might be assumed. Jung believed in having uninterrupted periods of two or three hours at a stretch in which he could think and reflect. Nothing must be allowed to interfere with this. Sometimes he would go to his house at Bollingen for a few days. There he would be undisturbed and unhurried. Apart from these breaks he was seeing patients regularly for some hours each day and the analysis of their dreams was of considerable value in what he described as *Confrontation with the Unconscious*.[104] This exacting work demanded resolution and energy. Progress was sometimes slow; but he knew the task—"my work with the unconscious"—must be accomplished. "Very gradually," he writes, "the outlines of an inner change began making their appearance within me."[105] This research continued for about three years, not, of course, to the total exclusion of outside activities. For instance in July 1914 he was invited to address the annual meeting of the British Medical Association at Aberdeen, where he read a paper *On the Importance of the Unconscious in Psychopathology*.[106]

Jung attached great importance to this period of facing the unconscious: "The essential thing is to differentiate oneself from these unconscious contents by personifying them and at the same time to bring them into relationship with consciousness. . . . All my works, all my creative activity, has come from those initial phantasies and dreams which began in 1912, almost fifty years ago. Everything that I accomplished in later life was already contained in them, although at first only in the form of emotions and images."[107]

In 1916 he wrote a short paper, *The Transcendent Function*, setting out his ideas on the problem: "How does one come to terms in practice with the unconscious?" Somehow this essay was put aside and it was not until 1953, on the initiative of the Students' Association, C. G. Jung Institute, Zürich, that it was published. Since then it has been reprinted in the Collected Works. In an Introductory Note Jung refers to the "unavoidable limitedness" of his work at that early stage (1916). Yet he felt the essay, with all its imperfections, "should stand as an historical document", because it gives an idea of the difficulties that had to be overcome in finding out how, and to what purpose, the conscious and the unconscious, as opposites, co-operated or collaborated to reach wholeness.[108]

In the early days Jung was aware that this study of the interaction of the conscious and unconscious had an effect on him, and he expressed this as a widening of consciousness. Later he saw that the change was in fact a continuous operation, or series of operations, in which he himself was involved, and eventually he described this as the process of individuation (p. 171). This term replaced the concept *transcendent function* which lacked the sense of continuity.

Individuation as a process involving self-regulation in the mind and the idea that life has a purpose are valuable concepts in the treatment of psychiatric illness. Thus in an obsessional neurosis, the symptoms seem designed to make life stand still and very little thought is given to the future. Likewise in states of depression, the tendency of the symptoms is to blot out the present by over-stating the importance of past events. It applies also in a third form of illness when both future and past are unwittingly obliterated because of a morbid pre-occupation with the problems of everyday life.

This three-fold division of symptoms does not mean that there are three rigidly separated groups of patients; as a rule the three groups overlap. They indicate, broadly, forms of personal maladjustment in which life as it exists, the current situation, is out of alignment with life as a process because the interplay of the conscious and unconscious is discordant rather than harmonious.

Emphasis upon the current problem did not prevent Jung from looking ahead. This was essential when national and international questions were affecting individuals all over the world. A tendency to assume that life will go on indefinitely, as we see it at this moment, is all too human. Jung was too much of a realist to accept such loose thinking. We must anticipate the future and we can only do so when we have a coherent picture of our individual outlook and feel that it must take account of the outlook and aims of other races and other countries.

THE UNDISCOVERED SELF

"What will the future bring?" These are the opening words of a notable book, written in 1956, and now included in Jung's Collected Works.[109] He asks this question as he surveys the scene of physical, political, economic and spiritual unrest and insecurity in Europe and in other countries. Perhaps we take it for granted that we know our own mind; but even this is more than doubtful. Nor are we really well acquainted with other people in their environment, although we may have an impression about them. There is then a "broad belt of unconsciousness, which is immune to conscious criticism and control and open to all kinds of influences". As these are unknown we cannot guard against them. How can we get to know the facts? Theories do not help much. The more a theory lays claim to universal validity, the less capable it is of doing justice to the individual facts. As such a theory is based on experience, "it is necessarily *statistical*; it formulates an *ideal average* . . . the exceptions at either extreme . . . do not appear in the final result at all, since they cancel each other out."[110] But it is these individual features we need if we are to understand man, hence "the real picture consists of nothing but exceptions to the rule".[111] Nevertheless man, as a member of a species, must be considered as a statistical unit "from which all individual features have been removed".

Yet we, as doctors, want to understand the individual man. So we get a clash between knowledge of man in the mass and understanding the individual. This conflict can only be solved "by a kind of two-way thinking: doing one thing while not losing sight of the other".[112] What appears to happen is "a levelling down and a process of blurring" that deprives the individual of his uniqueness and he is swept along in the policy of the State. More and more the individual loses his distinctiveness and he "is increasingly deprived of the moral decision as to how he should live his own life".[113]

Jung's claim was that ". . . all socio-political movements . . . invariably try to cut the ground from under *religion*. For in order to turn the individual into a function of the State, his dependence on anything else must be taken from him. . . ." Religion gives, or claims to give, a point of reference outside external conditions. Without such a point of reference the individual cannot have an attitude, a state of mind leading to action, in which judgment and powers of decision can be exercised.

Jung draws a distinction between a "creed" and a "religion". "A creed gives expression to a definite collective belief, whereas the word *religion* expresses a subjective relationship to certain metaphysical, extra-mundane factors . . . while the meaning and purpose of religion lie in the relationship of the individual to God

(Christianity, Judaism, Islam) or to the path of salvation and liberation (Buddhism)."[114]

Jung's critical study of the world situation today is put forward in all modesty, as that of "a psychiatrist who in the course of a long life has devoted himself to the causes and consequences of psychic disorders . . . I am neither spurred on by excessive optimism nor in love with high ideals, but am merely concerned with the fate of the individual human being—that infinitesimal unit on whom a world depends, and in whom, if we read the meaning of the Christian message aright, even God seeks his goal".[115]

What can this last sentence mean? Jung often mentions God in this book and elsewhere. We are reminded of a B.B.C. *Face to Face* Broadcast in 1959. In answer to a question, "Do you believe in God?" he replied, "I do not need to believe in God; I *know*." At once Jung was inundated with letters, many assuming that his belief in "God" corresponded with their own; others expressed disbelief in "God" and some wanted to know what he meant by "God" anyway. Unable to reply to his numerous correspondents Jung set out his views in the following letter to *The Listener*, January 21, 1960.

"Sir,—So many letters I have received have emphasized my statement about 'knowing' (of God) [in 'Face to Face', *The Listener*, October 29]. My opinion about 'knowledge of God' is an unconventional way of thinking, and I quite understand if it should be suggested that I am no Christian. Yet I think of myself as a Christian since I am entirely based upon Christian concepts. I only try to escape their internal contradictions by introducing a more modest attitude, which takes into consideration the immense darkness of the human mind. The Christian idea proves its vitality by a continuous evolution, just like Buddhism. Our time certainly demands some new thought in this respect, as we cannot continue to think in an antique or medieval way, when we enter the sphere of religious experience.

I did not say in the broadcast, 'There is a God.' I said, 'I do not need to believe in God; I *know*.' Which does not mean: I do know a certain God (Zeus, Jahwe, Allah, the Trinitarian God, etc.) but rather: I do know that I am obviously confronted with a factor unknown in itself, which I call 'God' in *consensu omnium* ('*quod semper, quod ubique, quod ab omnibus creditur*'). I remember Him, I evoke Him, whenever I use His name overcome by anger or by fear, whenever I involuntarily say: 'Oh God.'

That happens when I meet somebody or something stronger than myself. It is an apt name given to all overpowering emotions in my own psychical system subduing my conscious will and usurping control over myself. This is the name by which I designate all things which cross my wilful path violently and recklessly, all things which upset my subjective views, plans, and intentions and change the course of my life for better or worse. In accordance with tradition I call the power of fate in this positive as well as negative aspect, and inasmuch as its origin is beyond my control, 'god', a 'personal god', since my fate means very much myself, particularly when it approaches me in the form of conscience as a *vox Dei*, with which I can even converse and argue. (We do and, at the same time, we know that we do. One is subject as well as object.)

Yet I should consider it an intellectual immorality to indulge in the belief that my view of a god is the universal, metaphysical Being of the confessions or 'philosophies'. I do neither commit the impertinence of a *hypostasis*, nor of an arrogant qualification such as: 'God can only be good.' Only my experience can be good or evil, but I know that the superior will is based upon a foundation which transcends human imagination. Since I *know* of my collision with a superior will in my own psychical system, *I know of God*, and if I should venture the illegitimate hypostasis of my image, I would say, of *a God beyond good and evil*, just as much dwelling in myself as everywhere else: *Deus est circulus cuius centrum est ubique, cuius circumferentia vero nusquam.*

Yours, etc.,

Zürich   CARL GUSTAV JUNG."

THE PERSONALITY AS A WHOLE: CONSCIOUS AND
UNCONSCIOUS

In face of threats to the individual, a responsibility falls on the psychotherapist—whose duty it is to deal with individuals—to enable his patient to free himself from the limitations of a purely ego-conscious outlook. With this expansion of his outlook to include the hidden unconscious parts of his personality, he should acquire "enough certainty of judgment to enable him to act on his own insight and decision and not from the mere wish to copy convention. . . ."[116]

When the ego-conscious personality, with its inadequate grasp of what it is capable of, is unable to cope with events there may be a nervous breakdown and childhood fantasies may reappear. They have been present all along but only became visible when the conscious resources proved unequal to the occasion. Development in the personality seems to stop and the patient is stuck at the stage of ego-consciousness. There has been no movement towards wholeness, because he has never been aware that the unconscious is a reality.

Our outlook should be representative of the total personality—the conscious and the unconscious—if we are to live fully in the world as individuals and not as cyphers. In effect this is a plea for sound preventive measures in order that mental health may be developed and retained. "Our ideas," says Jung, "have the unfortunate but inevitable tendency to lag behind the changes in the total situation. . . ." In such a situation "the analyst has to establish a relationship with both halves of his patient's personality, because only from them can be put together a whole and complete man".[117]

When man gets separated from his instinctual nature, he is plunged inevitably into the conflict between his conscious life and the world of the unconscious—his undiscovered self. A prevailing tendency in our age is to seek the cause of all ills in the outside world. Hence mass movements. But this can never solve the deeper problems of the divided personality. "Yet," says Jung, "we think that psychic mistakes and their consequences can be got rid of with mere words, for 'psychic' means less than air to most people. All the same, nobody can deny that without the psyche there would be no world at all, and still less a human world."[118]

INDIVIDUATION AS A PROCESS. THE SELF

As the unconscious is always unknown until we make it conscious, sometimes it is assumed that conscious life represents the entire psyche or mind. A little experience of dream-analysis soon brings a changed outlook and the patient discovers through his own experience that the mind, conscious and unconscious, is wider than he had thought. Jung introduced the term *individuation* "to denote the process by which a person becomes a psychological 'in-dividual', that is a separate, indivisible unity or 'whole'".[119]

It is necessary to distinguish individualism, which represents a self-centred notion of free and independent action and thought, from individuation, which means bringing to fulfilment the collective as well as the personal qualities of the person. Individuation, as a process, can be seen at important stages in life and at times of crisis when fate upsets the purpose and expectation of the ego-consciousness. By its unaided efforts the ego-conscious personality cannot bring the complete man to our awareness; usually this requires a joint effort of consciousness and the unconscious. In other words, the one-sidedness of conscious life is corrected, compensated for, by the interaction of the conscious and unconscious. This describes the striving for fulfilment which, Jung believes, is inherent in everyone. This may never be accomplished; but it is the aim of the process of individuation. Man operates with design and purpose; he has a goal in sight. This is brought nearer not by what we intend to do, but in the actual way in which life is lived and inborn capacities realised. Often life is lived inadequately and hopes are disappointed. Success in the full sense requires the union of the opposites. That is, when the process of individuation takes place the combination of the conscious and unconscious leads to the assimilation of the ego in a wider personality, described as the *self*. Jung spoke of it in these words: "It is the whole, conscious and unconscious, what I myself am, and it involves much we do not know is there, for instance our body and its workings and the unconscious."

Jung elaborates the concept of individuation: ". . . This process is, in effect, the spontaneous realization of the whole man. . . . The more he is merely 'I', the more he splits himself off from the collective man, of whom he is also a part, and may even find himself in opposition to him. But since everything living strives for wholeness, the inevitable one-sidedness of our conscious life is continually being corrected and compensated by the universal human being in us, whose goal is the ultimate integration of conscious and unconscious, or better, the assimilation of the ego to a wider personality."[120]

Individuation is thus a process of integration of the world of consciousness and the inner world of the unconscious. Such action and reaction is inherent in development and growth, and this is the meaning of the process. In the course of a lifetime we pass through a series of changes. To begin with conscious life emerges from the background of the unconscious. An infant is aware that something is going on around him, although he has not reached the stage of recognising himself as a separate entity, as "I". That is why infants and young children take it for granted that others know their point of view. Consciousness is not continuous in the child's waking life; there are patches, islands of consciousness, gradually emerging from unawareness and, for years, an unawareness of itself as an individual. In later adolescence and through the first half of life a differentiation of the ego takes place. As middle-life is reached and the years pass, subjective life is (or should be) enlarged, because a process of development has occurred. A mature attitude towards life has come about and the immaturity of ego-consciousness has given place to a natural—probably unnoticed— acceptance of the collective background of life. Delayed acceptance of responsibility for one's life stands out in contrast to mature development. In healthy people there is a shift in the centre of gravity of the personality and the ego is superseded by a less ego-centred, that is a non-personal or not exclusively personal centre—the self. Since our conscious life came originally from the unconscious and passes gradually to the development of ego-consciousness, this in turn leads or tends to lead through the appreciation of the non-ego towards the experience of relatedness, to the wholeness of life. Individuation implies a living relation between the conscious and unconscious. This aim is inherent in life, an ideal reached through the process of blending personal and collective interests. These complement one another to form a totality, the self. "It transcends our powers of imagination to form a clear picture of what we are as a self, for in this operation the part would have to comprehend the whole. . . . But the more we become conscious of ourselves, through self-knowledge, and act accordingly, the more the layer of the personal unconscious that is superimposed on the collective unconscious will be diminished. In this way there arises a consciousness which is no longer imprisoned in the petty, oversensitive, personal world of the ego, but participates freely in the wider world of objective interests. The complications . . . are no longer egotistic wish-conflicts, but difficulties that concern others as much as oneself. . . . We can now see that the unconscious produces contents which are valid not only for the person concerned, but for others as well, in fact for a great many people and possibly for all."[121]

Throughout his long career Jung maintained a remarkable degree of open-mindedness. He expected change and welcomed it as a sign of healthy expansion. Most of his central ideas, such as his hypothesis of the collective unconscious, changed and developed during his time. Had he lived longer other changes would have come. In the treatment of patients he always showed an expectant interest. This is true of his system of thought. He excluded the limitations of dogma and confidently anticipated progress.

Looking to the future of Analytical Psychology, Jung, in the Foreword to a book[122] by one of his pupils, writes: ". . . how great are the disadvantages of pioneer work: one stumbles through unknown regions . . . forever losing the Ariadne thread; one is overwhelmed by new impressions and new possibilities. . . . The second generation has the advantage of a clearer, if still incomplete, picture; certain landmarks that at least lie on the frontiers of the essential have grown familiar, and one now knows what must be known if one is to explore the newly discovered territory."

REFERENCES

FOREWORD

1. *Types,* p. 530.

CHAPTER I

2. C.W., Vol. 1, p. 3.
3. M.D.R., p. 111.
4. BBC Broadcast, 1955. Quoted in C.G.J., p. 147.
5. C.W., Vol. 8, p. 99.
6. *ibid.,* pp. 96–97.
7. C.W., Vol. 10, p. 544.
8. Jones, Ernest, *Sigmund Freud—Life and Work* (London: Hogarth Press, 1955), II, 48, 53. Published in the U.S. by Basic Books, New York, under the title, *The Life and Work of Sigmund Freud.*
9. C.W., Vol. 3, p. 3.

10. BBC Broadcast, 1955. Quoted in C.G.J., p. 148.
11. M.D.R., p. 146.

CHAPTER 2

12. M.D.R., p. 147.
13. *ibid.*, pp. 147–48.
14. *Types*, p. 601.
15. Jung, C. G., *Contributions to Analytical Psychology* (London: Kegan Paul, Trench, Trubner & Co. Ltd., 1928), pp. 231–32. Re-published in C.W. as Vol. 15, *The Spirit in Man, Art, and Literature.*
16. Dalbiez, Roland, *Psychoanalytic Method and the Doctrine of Freud* (London: Longmans, Green & Co., Ltd.), II, 102–3.
17. M.D.R., p. 162.
18. C.W., Vol. 5, chap. VIII.
19. *ibid.*, p. 420.
20. Jones, *op. cit.*, II, 165.
21. M.D.R., p. 153.
22. *ibid.*, p. 153.
23. Wittels, Fritz, *Sigmund Freud, His Personality, His Teaching and His School* (London: Allen & Unwin, 1924), p. 178.
24. C.W., Vol. 4, "Freud and Jung: Contrasts," pp. 334–35, 337–38.
25. C.W., Vol. 7, pp. 40–43.
26. *ibid.*, p. 272.
27. *ibid.*, p. 273.
28. *Types*, p. 10.
29. *ibid.*, p. 14.
30. *ibid.*, p. 547.

CHAPTER 3

31. M.D.R., pp. 163–64.

32. C.W., Vol. 3, p. 211.
33. *ibid.*, p. 233.
34. *ibid.*, p. 250.
35. *ibid.*, p. 253.
36. C.W., Vol. 11, pp. 14–15.
37. C.W., Vol. 9, Part I, pp. 43–44.
38. *ibid.*, p. 4.
39. Frankfort, Henri, "The Archetype in Analytical Psychology and the History of Religion," *Journal of the Warburg and Courtauld Institutes* (1958), Vol. XXI, Nos. 3–4, pp. 166–78.
40. C.W., Vol. 9, Part I, pp. 3–5.
41. *ibid.*, p. 78.
42. Stafford-Clark, David, *What Freud Really Said* (London: Macdonald, 1965), p. 236. (New York: Schocken Books, 1966.)
43. M.D.R., p. 154.
44. Jones, *op. cit.*, II, 165.
45. C.G.J., pp. 86–87.
46. M.D.R., p. 155.
47. C.G.J., p. 88.
48. M.S., p. 38.
49. Freud, Sigmund, *An Autobiographical Study* (London: Hogarth Press, 1949), p. 121. (New York: W. W. Norton, 1963.)
50. C.G.J., p. 102.
51. Toynbee, Arnold J., *Civilization on Trial* (London and New York: Oxford University Press, 1949), p. 11.
52. C.W., Vol. 8, p. 150.
53. C.W., Vol. 5, p. 102.

CHAPTER 4

54. C.G.J., p. 10.
55. C.W., Vol. 16, p. 151.
56. *ibid.*, p. 142.

57. *ibid.,* p. 158.
58. M.S., p. 78.
59. M.D.R., p. 291.
60. C.W., Vol. 8, p. 255.
61. C.W., Vol. 7, p. 178.
62. C.W., Vol. 8, p. 291.

CHAPTER 5

63. C.W., Vol. 17, p. 65.
64. *ibid.,* pp. 67–68.
65. C.W., Vol. 8, p. 349.
66. Jung, C. G., "Fundamental Psychological Conceptions." Seminar given in London, 1935. Pp. 217–18.
67. C.W., Vol. 16, pp. 45–46.
68. C.W., Vol. 14, p. 248.
69. *ibid.,* p. 320.
70. *Studien zur Analytischen Psychologie C. G. Jungs,* (Zürich: Rascher, 1955). Vol. I, "The Double," by E. A. Bennett, pp. 384–96.
71. *Types,* p. 590.
72. C.W., Vol. 9, Part I, pp. 8–9.
73. *ibid.,* pp. 83, 85.
74. *ibid.,* p. 30.
75. C.W., Vol. 9, Part II, p. 10.
76. C.W., Vol. 7, pp. 186–88.
77. C.W., Vol. 17, p. 199.
78. *ibid.,* p. 198.
79. C.W., Vol. 11, pp. 30–31.
80. C.W., Vol. 9, Part II, p. 268.
81. Jung, Emma, *Animus and Anima,* p. 87.
82. C.W., Vol. 7, p. 207.

CHAPTER 6

83. M.D.R., p. 113.

84. *ibid.*, p. 121.
85. *ibid.*, p. 131.
86. *ibid.*, p. 158.
87. C.W., Vol. 16, p. 37.
88. C.W., Vol. 7, p. 45.
89. *ibid.*, p. 62.
90. C.W., Vol. 16, p. 164.
91. *ibid.*, p. 165.
92. *ibid.*, p. 166.
93. M.D.R., p. 203.
94. C.W., Vol. 16, p. 116.
95. Jung, C. G., "Fundamental Psychological Conceptions," p. 173.
96. C.W., Vol. 16, p. 233.
97. M.D.R., p. 194.
98. *ibid.*, p. 195.
99. *ibid.*, pp. 196–97.
100. C.W., Vol. 12, pp. 36–37.
101. C.W., Vol. 7, p. 218.
102. C.W., Vol. 10, pp. 184–85.
103. C.W., Vol. 8, pp. 395–96.

CHAPTER 7

104. M.D.R., chap. VI, p. 165.
105. *ibid.*, p. 182.
106. C.W., Vol. 3, p. 203.
107. M.D.R., pp. 179, 184.
108. C.W., Vol. 8, p. 67.
109. C.W., Vol. 10, p. 247.
110. *ibid.*, p. 249.
111. *ibid.*, p. 250.
112. *ibid.*, p. 251.
113. *ibid.*, p. 252.
114. *ibid.*, pp. 256–57.

115. *ibid.*, p. 305.
116. *ibid.*, p. 275.
117. *ibid.*, pp. 284, 286.
118. *ibid.*, p. 291.
119. C.W., Vol. 9, Part I, p. 275.
120. C.W., Vol. 8, p. 292.
121. C.W., Vol. 7, pp. 175–76.
122. Neumann, Erich, *The Origins and History of Consciousness,* with a Foreword by C. G. Jung (London: Routledge and Kegan Paul Ltd., 1954). (New York: Bollingen Foundation, 1954.)

INDEX